GUI

CW00539734

'Cato' was the pseudonym used ... journalists who wrote *Guilty Men*. They were Peter Howard, a columnist for the *Sunday Express* and ex-captain of England's rugby team, Frank Owen, editor of the *Evening Standard* and military historian, and Michael Foot, then also writing for the *Evening Standard*.

The Right Honourable Michael Foot became editor of the *Evening Standard* in 1942 and subsequently of the *Tribune*. He entered Parliament in 1945 as MP for Devonport and on his retirement from the House in 1992 had been MP for Blaenau Gwent for nine years. He was Leader of the Labour Party for the period 1980–83. He is the author of a number of other books, the most recent being *H. G.: The History of Mr Wells* (1995).

John Stevenson was born in 1946 and read History at Worcester College, Oxford. He has taught at Oriel College, Oxford, and the University of Sheffield, and is currently Fellow and Tutor in History at Worcester College. As well as writing the introduction to this new edition of *Guilty Men* he has written a number of books on history, society and politics, including *British Society 1914-45* (Penguin, 1984).

(10) £2.49

GUILTY MEN

'CATO'

PENGUIN BOOKS

PENGUIN BOOKS

Published by the Penguin Group
Penguin Books Ltd, 27 Wrights Lane, London w8 5tz, England
Penguin Putnam Inc., 375 Hudson Street, New York, New York 10014, USA
Penguin Books Australia Ltd, Ringwood, Victoria, Australia
Penguin Books Canada Ltd, 10 Alcorn Avenue, Toronto, Ontario, Canada m4v 3b2
Penguin Books (NZ) Ltd, 182–190 Wairau Road, Auckland 10, New Zealand

Penguin Books Ltd, Registered Offices: Harmondsworth, Middlesex, England

First published by Victor Gollancz 1940
Published with a new preface and introduction in Penguin Books 1998
1 3 5 7 9 10 8 6 4 2

Preface to the Penguin edition copyright © Michael Foot, 1998
Introduction to the Penguin edition copyright © John Stevenson, 1998
All rights reserved

The moral right of the authors of the preface and introduction to
the Penguin edition has been asserted

Printed in England by Clays Ltd, St Ives plc

Except in the United States of America, this book is sold subject
to the condition that it shall not, by way of trade or otherwise, be lent,
re-sold, hired out, or otherwise circulated without the publisher's
prior consent in any form of binding or cover other than that in
which it is published and without a similar condition including this
condition being imposed on the subsequent purchaser

PREFACE TO THE PENGUIN EDITION

BY MICHAEL FOOT

Guilty Men was conceived by three London journalists who had formed the habit of meeting on the roof of the *Evening Standard* offices in Shoe Lane, Fleet Street, just after the afternoon paper had been put to bed and, maybe, just before the Two Brewers opened across the road. On the roof, no one could overhear what we were saying to one another, but it was also the place where we might remind ourselves what might happen to our city and our country. The term 'Guilty Men' was the one which achieved particular fame, quite unforeseen by us – come to that, and to the particular writers in a moment. The scene and the moment are significant.

July 1940 was the finest month in that finest, unforgettable year. Looking back now, we may reckon that the finest *hour*, to use the term literally, had occurred a little earlier when Chamberlain was slung out and Churchill was put in his place, although Churchill himself did not, immodestly, apply the word thus. His happy compliment was intended for the British people and their performance.

I well remember the London of that July: how the sun blazed more brilliantly each day, how the green parks, the whole city indeed, had never looked lovelier. All of us who lived through those times had a special instruction in the meaning of patriotism. The sense of the community in which we had been born and bred suffused all else, made everything else subordinate or trivial. And one essential element in the exhilaration was the knowledge that the shameful Chamberlain era had at last been brought to an end, and that English people could look into each other's eyes with recovered pride and courage.

If anyone questions this last seemingly exaggerated claim, I would refer him to the verdict passed by one of the very greatest journalist-observers of our century. Rebecca West wrote an epilogue to her classic, *Black Lamb and Grey Falcon*, a book about other people's patriotism to be published a year later. She thought the stain of what Chamberlain's England had done to the Czechs and the Poles could never be wiped away, but she expressed too the sense of cleansing liberation which enabled London and later the whole country to survive all the trials ahead.

With unrelenting crudity, without a scrap of Rebecca West's style, and with nothing to recommend it in a literary sense but red-hot topicality, a book was published that July which purported to describe how the nation had been thrust into such a critical condition and what remedies were needed to save us. It was called *Guilty Men*, and maybe, despite the glaring defects in the text itself, the title did have a touch of salesman's genius. It sold like a pornographic classic, especially in bookstalls round Leicester Square and especially when regular bookstalls sought to ban it. Being one of the authors, I can testify that the whole affair was contrived in a rush and a rage: our aim was to secure changes in the men running the war. I could hardly have expected that half a century later it would be the subject of detailed historical analysis.

Guilty Men's argument about how Britain became engulfed in the Second World War became the Churchill argument too. Indeed *Guilty Men* quoted Churchill on its cover, and he took a genial view of the exposition at the time. His own post-war volume, *The Gathering Storm*, described the events as 'the unnecessary war'; and three of his leading culprits, Baldwin, Chamberlain and Halifax, also headed the *Guilty Men* list. Two of them, as we now learn, although no outsiders knew at the time, favoured some fresh deal with Hitler and Mussolini, some fresh infamies, according to the Rebecca West test, in that same blazing summer.

However, despite Churchill's prestige both as war leader and historian, despite his strange or interested alliance with the scurrilous *Guilty Men* authors, the theory did not stand unchallenged. Gradually, the Revisionists of one school or another got to work. Had not those who made the deal with Hitler and Mussolini made possible the essential British rearmament from which Churchill was to profit? Individual biographers of the particular miscreants shared a happy knack of unloosing some of the guilt on their fellow victims in the dock. Fanciful theories were devised to suggest that the time bought by Chamberlain saved the country in the later struggle. Munich was presented not as a surrender, but as a brilliant stratagem.

Then suddenly, in the early 1960s, a new Revision in a new direction by a real historian dazzled all beholders. A. J. P. Taylor ransacked the origins of the war in the diplomatic archives and offered a more sophisticated analysis than either the Churchillites or the Chamberlainites had supplied. Robert Boyce, the editor of the most important new study on the subject, *Paths to War*, published by Macmillan in 1990, asserts in his introduction that 'Taylor remains the master speculator in this field', and, considering the tumult of debate which had raged back and forth on every aspect of the theme, that is a mighty commendation indeed.

One reason why the Taylor thesis has stood up so well

to so much buffeting may be that it was never the apology for appeasement which his critics chose to claim. His Baldwin, Chamberlain and Halifax meant well with their pious self-righteous protestations; but in every crisis they behaved like ignoramuses or poltroons or cowards. Our enemies drew the conclusion that the British people were made from the same mould, and would act with the same pusillanimity. Nineteen-forty taught them how wrong they were.

Mostly, the new excellent series of essays, edited by Robert Boyce, had the effect of revising the Revisionists, a salutary requirement when we recall that a recent supposedly serious study of Churchill's 1940 conduct, seen from the Chamberlain camp, suggested that the real question is whether he and the rest of the nation should not have given in, as Chamberlain and Halifax still advised as late as the winter of that year.

However, here at last, as MPs sometimes say, I must declare an interest. The most original essay in the book, by Sidney Aster, Professor of History at the University of Toronto, tackles the neglected question about whether the most modern available evidence, especially from Chamberlain's own diaries, confirms the indictment of *Guilty Men*.

A note on my two fellow authors and, even more necessary, on our common proprietor, or the casual reader might think I was engaged in some interested concealment. Not so, as Beaverbrook, the proprietor concerned, might himself say, or Peter Howard, one of the authors, might himself say. Peter wrote every Sunday in the *Sunday Express* the column which many experts thought most directly reflected Beaverbrook's own views. He had other claims to fame. He had been born with a deformed ankle-bone which looked as if it might snap at any moment, and yet he had survived to captain England at Rugby. Beaverbrook had certainly played his part in making Peter a good journalist.

Frank Owen, the other part-author of *Guilty Men*, owed several debts to Beaverbrook too, but he had his own touch of journalistic genius which would have taken him to the top anywhere. He was the editor of the *Evening Standard* who could inspire the whole staff but he was one of those rare editors who could turn his hand to any other kind of journalism. He seemed especially qualified to edit a newspaper in wartime, having been trained as a military historian and having attracted to the *Standard* an extraordinary array of military experts headed by Liddel Hart and J. F. C. Fuller. Whatever else could be scoffed at, the military assessments had their basis in his deep understanding of the subject.

Beaverbrook himself had no knowledge of our meetings on the roof of the *Evening Standard* building, which was one of the reasons why we held them there. At the time of the publication, he was fully engaged as the new Minister of Aircraft Production in the new Churchill Government. Normally, he would be in touch with his editors every day. He was fascinated by journalism himself, more indeed a super-editor than a modern proprietor. For whole weeks on end throughout May, June and July of 1940, this mode of communication was suspended. He must have at first been mystified by a production in which some of the style was so familiar and where he himself seemed to be protected from criticism – strange rumours were spread about who 'Cato' might be, some spread, I must confess, from the *Standard* office. A lengthy list of eligible anti-Munichites was available – Randolph Churchill, son of Winston, or Duff Cooper, who had resigned from the Chamberlain government at

the time of Munich – these and several more. My own
critical review of the book in the *Standard* book page
helped distract attention. After a while, the notion of a
composite work added to the guesswork.

How long it took Beaverbrook himself to make the dis-
covery, we never knew, but some months later an authen-
tic conversation was recorded between two members of
Churchill's Cabinet who hardly ever exchanged a civil
word. Lord Halifax remarked to Lord Beaverbrook how
difficult it must be for a millionaire like him to live on a
Cabinet minister's salary. 'Indeed,' replied Beaverbrook,
'but I make do, you know, with the royalties from *Guilty
Men.*'

Before, during and after the actual publication in July,
Chamberlain was writing in his diary the incriminating
confessions which proved that he still did not understand
what the menace of Hitlerism meant for our country and
how his actions had contributed to the peril. If this evidence had been available it would have clinched our case;
indeed, outraged Londoners would have been besieging
Chamberlain's house in London.

MICHAEL FOOT
August 1997

INTRODUCTION
TO THE PENGUIN EDITION

BY JOHN STEVENSON

No government, perhaps since the days of Lord North and the loss of the American Colonies, has been so widely criticized and scorned as that of Neville Chamberlain. Its reputation rose and fell with the policy of appeasement: greeted as the hero of the hour at the time of the Munich Agreement in the autumn of 1938, Chamberlain was to find himself vilified as the man who had brought the nation close to disaster as an ill-prepared country found itself harried from defeat to defeat in the spring and early summer of 1940. Chamberlain's resignation as Prime Minister on 10 May 1940 following a backbench revolt over the handling of the Norwegian campaign and his replacement by Churchill at the head of an all-party coalition has been seen not only as a turning-point in the conduct of the Second World War, but also as tantamount to a national deliverance. A new administration, fired by the energy and rhetoric of Churchill – the man who almost alone had stood out for resistance to the dictators and for urgent rearmament – was now committed to the vigorous and resolute prosecution of the war at almost any cost. By the same token, almost a decade of complacency and mismanagement which had brought the country to the brink of catastrophe and placed it in dire peril was laid at the door of those in charge of pre-war foreign policy. That indictment found definitive shape in the blistering polemic published by Gollancz in early July 1940 as *Guilty Men*.

Using as its motto the words used by Churchill in 1936, 'The use of recriminating about the past is to enforce effective action at the present,' *Guilty Men* took as its opening scene 'The Beaches of Dunkirk'. Writing with the memory only a few days old of the epic evacuation of over 330,000 men of the British Expeditionary Force and the allied forces, at the cost of most of their guns, tanks and heavy equipment, the question was posed: 'How was it that the bravest sons of Britain ever came to be placed in such jeopardy?' 'Various, complicated answers' were set aside for 'an-other answer more truthful and more comprehensive . . . the answer stuttered out by every soldier as he stepped ashore'; the answer was to be found in the story of an heroic battle against superior odds, tanks, planes and equipment – 'Unconquerable spirit against overpowering weapons' – 'the story of an Army doomed *before* they took the field'.

Accordingly, *Guilty Men* sought the culprits for the calamity of the retreat from Belgium and the near-disaster of Dunkirk amongst those in power in the previous decade. A succession of either supine or deluded leaders, MacDonald, Baldwin and, above all, Chamberlain, abetted by lesser ministers, and their cohorts of admirers and yes-men, had failed to take heed of the threats posed by the dictators or, when alerted, had failed to awaken the public to the dangers that faced them. Concession after concession had been made in order to avoid difficult and compromising decisions; appeasement, begun as a policy of legitimate remedy of Germany's grievances over the Treaty of Versailles, became a policy of abject surrender of position after position in the face of the aggressive acts or threats from Hitler or his lesser rival Mussolini. The Rhineland was reoccupied, Germany permitted to build an airforce and to introduce conscription, all in defiance

of the Treaty of Versailles, without a finger being raised.
By the Anglo-German Naval agreement, Britain openly
set aside the clauses that had prevented Germany building large capital ships and possessing a submarine fleet.
Mussolini was allowed, in spite of ineffective League of
Nations sanctions, to gobble up Abyssinia, and both
Hitler and Mussolini permitted to provide crucial assistance to Franco's assault on the Spanish Republic.
Meanwhile, France and Britain pursued a policy of 'non-
intervention' effectively leaving the Spanish government
to certain and ultimate defeat. The *Anschluss* with Austria
was to be followed by the surrender of the Czech
Sudetenland to Hitler's bullying aggression. There, for a
time, it appeared that peace had been snatched from the
jaws of war. Chamberlain returned from his second visit
to Hitler in triumph, promising 'peace in our time'. But
peace, many already felt, had been bought at too high a
price; whether in terms of international morality, betray-
ing the Czechs and bullying them into concessions they
could only see as the dismemberment of their newly-
formed state, or, simply, of *realpolitik*, not only yielding
once again to Hitlerite aggression but surrendering one of
the most strongly fortified frontiers in Europe and an ally
both determined and equipped to defend it. But the illusion of peace was soon to be shattered by Hitler's brutal
and callous disregard for the agreement signed at
Munich. On 15 March 1939 German troops crossed the
Czech frontier and marched on Prague. President Hacha
was forced into an agreement making Moravia and
Bohemia 'protectorates' of Germany.

Germany's forced dismemberment of the Czech
Republic without a sign of effective response by the
Western Allies was followed by what the authors of *Guilty
Men* saw as a bizarre step, a guarantee to Poland which

virtually placed the decision of war or peace in the hands of the Poles or, according to the authors, in the hands of a 'country ruled by a degenerate crew of landowners and old soldiers'. Not only were the Poles on notoriously bad terms with the Soviets, an ally which Britain needed desperately to win to her side, but also they had participated in the destruction of Czechoslovakia, seizing the enclave of Teschen. Moreover, the Poles were virtually impossible to assist. It was evident to everyone that no branch of the British armed forces had the capacity to bring direct aid to Poland in the event of German aggression. When Lloyd George asked in the Commons if the General Staff had agreed to the acceptance of the guarantee of a frontier in the east of Europe which we could not easily reach and when we had no Allies who could reach it, he received no answer.

Further, as *Guilty Men* argued, even with a firm commitment to assist the Poles the necessary preparations for war were not undertaken. A succession of incompetent and unsuitable ministers was appointed to oversee rearmament and the departments of state necessary to running a successful war economy. Damning a succession of these appointments, *Guilty Men* fulminated at Chamberlain's pledges to adopt vigorous and responsible measures at the time of the guarantee to Poland, contrasting them bitterly with the actual record over the sixteen months leading up to the Dunkirk evacuation. As a result the lives of those lost in the first months of the war were the responsibility of the appeasers. Hence 'every British airman killed in this war, every British civilian killed by Nazi bombers, every little child in the kingdom who may be robbed of life and happiness . . .' was to have as an epitaph the reassuring platitudes of Baldwin in the mid-1930s that Britain would never allow Germany superiority over herself in armaments. Instead complacency and self-deception had ruled, bolstered by a large Commons majority, mercilessly forced into line by the Chief Whip, Captain David Margesson, and frequently ready to employ the ostracism and denigration of its critics, notably Churchill.

Published only a month after the evacuation from Dunkirk and a fortnight after the fall of France when Britain stood alone and terrifyingly weak in the face of an imminent German invasion, *Guilty Men* was a highly charged rendering of the catalogue of events which had brought Britain to one of the gravest crises in its history. It captured something of the savage, almost vindictive, mood of a country which felt betrayed by its former leaders. The 'cast list' of the indictment comprised major, and some minor, figures of the pre-war administrations including some still serving under the Churchill coalition. It included almost everyone who could be cited for responsibility for Britain's predicament from Prime Ministers down through those responsible for major departments, and the long-standing government Chief Whip. *Guilty Men* ended with a ringing declaration that while the Churchill Government was repairing the 'breaches in our walls' it should not 'carry along with them those who let the walls fall into ruin'. Rather, 'Let the Guilty Men retire, then, of their own volition, and so make an essential contribution to the victory upon which all are implacably resolved.'

That *Guilty Men* caught a genuine tide of opinion was evident from its sales. Although not handled by the regular book distributors, W. H. Smith and Wyman's, it sold 50,000 copies in a few days, 200,000 copies by the end of the year, and went through twenty-one impressions in

eleven weeks. Its publisher, Victor Gollancz, was already
well-known as the enterprising founder of the Left Book
Club, which had attracted over 60,000 subscribers in the
years leading up to the war. Oriented well to the Left of
Centre, its choices of two new books each month had
reflected the growing preoccupation of a wide spectrum
of the British Left with anti-fascism, especially the plight
of the Spanish Republic and the fate of the eastern
European states threatened, if not already overwhelmed,
by the Nazis. *Guilty Men* was the first of a new series of
'Victory Books' with future titles promised on *The People's
War*, *Enlist India for Freedom* and *Churchill Can Unite Ireland*.
Guilty Men thus found its publisher and its milieu on the
Left, though as employees of Beaverbrook the three
journalists concerned could scarcely be written off as
unthinking 'fellow-travellers' and toadies of the latest
Moscow 'line'. None the less, the provenance of *Guilty
Men* clearly had some effect on the reviews it received, as
did the perception that 'rocking the boat' at a time of
national crisis was neither desirable nor necessary. *The
Times Literary Supplement* in a short notice certainly caught
the essence of Cato's bitterest recrimination:

> That a democracy should be less prepared for war than a
> totalitarian State is unfortunately inevitable but the point of
> 'Cato's' indictment is that to be so far behind at the outset
> and, still worse, to regain so little lost ground during nine
> months of actual warfare points to culpable weakness of
> leadership.

But the *TLS* argued against a purge on two grounds:

> In the first place it is a little difficult to see how either
> the unity of the nation or the efficiency of the administration
> would benefit by a sweeping proscription, which would cer-

tainly follow party divisions. Secondly, to turn upon 'guilty men' is neither quite fair to the statesmen in question nor healthy for the nation. The English people as a whole are only less guilty than their leaders, and to obscure their own responsibility by blaming the Government would be to fall into a fatal error of Democracy.[1]

The *Spectator* also gave *Guilty Men* only a short notice. While recognizing it as 'lively reading' and 'fortified by many quotations that the speakers would probably wish to forget', it felt it 'unfair' of 'Cato' to blame his 'cast list' for all the misfortunes of the B.E.F. in France. The truth of the central allegation, however, was accepted: that successive ministers were deceived by Hitler and, when undeceived, failed to apply themselves with sufficient vigour to remedy the situation. But the final note of the review was negative and not untypical of other responses: 'It is difficult to see how a revival of the controversy about Munich and other disappointing episodes, and a sort of Pride's Purge, will help us to get on with the war.'[2]

A warmer welcome came from the *New Statesman*, in a paragraph in its 'London Diary', but with its own distinctive spin to the ball. 'Cato' had not considered 'how far we are all guilty nor does he attempt any deep analysis of the social forces that have brought us to this pass'. While the individuals indicted by 'Cato' were undoubtedly responsible for incompetence and delusion, they were also 'the chief political representatives of a dying plutocracy which tried to maintain itself by manipulating a democratic constitution in its own interests'. They were 'the servants of a system; they could not in the nature of things realise that it was defunct; they had not the imagination to see the need of a new social order.' But blame was widely shared, according to the reviewer, and 'guilt' was inappropriate when what was needed was to displace unsuitable ministers and avoid the tragic conflict of policies which had led to the débâcle in France.[3]

The relatively cool reception of *Guilty Men* in the heavyweight periodicals was counterbalanced by its evident popularity with the general public. At a stroke *Guilty Men* set an agenda for the debate on appeasement which was to rage into the post-war years. No tract on foreign policy since Keynes's *Economic Consequences of the Peace* in 1919, damning the reparations clauses of the Treaty of Versailles, had so decisively seared itself into the public consciousness. But with the benefit of hindsight it can be seen as a tract for the times in more senses than one. As well as a brilliant indictment of appeasement, its immediate political context was an attempt to complete the work begun on 10 May with the replacement of Chamberlain by Churchill by a complete sweep from government of those responsible for the conduct of foreign policy up to that point. Although the advent of Churchill and a coalition government could be seen as a landmark in the prosecution of the war, the political scenario was more complicated than it might appear at first sight, stemming in large part from the circumstances and nature of the events that brought Churchill to power. The failure of the Norwegian campaign had allowed Labour to turn the debate into a vote of confidence in the Government. The ensuing debate finally unmuzzled enough Conservative hostility to lead to severe attacks upon the leadership even from its own benches. Even so, Chamberlain had a majority of 81 (281 for: 200 against), but 41 of those who usually supported the Government voted with the Opposition, while 60 more abstained. This loss of support mortally wounded the Chamberlain administration and attempts to win over the Conservative rebels foundered when they refused to join a government unless Labour and Liberals were brought in. As neither Labour nor the Liberals would serve under Chamberlain, it quickly became apparent that somebody else would have to lead the government. The initial and most obvious choice was Halifax, but his reluctance as a peer to be Prime Minister 'in such a war as this' was sufficient to give Churchill the premiership. From the outset, then, Churchill was Prime Minister almost by default.[4] In reality, a large number of Conservative MPs mistrusted Churchill and for many he would have been only third choice, at best, as leader of the country. John Colville, Private Secretary to Chamberlain and subsequently to Churchill, confided to his diary on 10 May:

He may, of course, be the man of drive and energy the country believes him to be and he may be able to speed up our creeking military and industrial machinery: but it is a terrible risk, it involves the danger of rash and spectacular exploits, and I cannot help fearing that this country may be manoeuvred into the most dangerous position it has ever been in.

Colville was in touch with other Conservatives who were even less restrained.

... I went over to the F.O. to explain the position to Rab [Butler], and there, with Chips [Channon], we drank in champagne to the health of the 'King over the Water' (not King Leopold, but Mr Chamberlain). Rab said ... he had tried earnestly and long to persuade Halifax to accept the Premiership, but he had failed. He believed this sudden coup of Winston and his rabble was a serious disaster and an unnecessary one: the 'pass had been sold' by Mr C., Lord Halifax and

Oliver Stanley. They had weakly surrendered to a half-breed American whose main support was that of inefficient but talkative people of a similar type . . .[5]

The advent of a new Premier and a coalition government had not by any means destroyed the influence and reputation of the previous administration, nor the parliamentary arithmetic which still gave Chamberlain a majority in the house. As A. J. P. Taylor commented:

Though Churchill had some faithful followers, in the last resort he succeeded by calling in the people against the men at the top. The words which he applied to Lloyd George were true of himself: 'He seized power. Perhaps the power was his to take.' Chamberlain was more generous than Asquith in December 1916 and agreed to serve under the man who had supplanted him. The Conservatives who had backed Chamberlain to the last did not forgive so easily. When the house met on 13 May, they rose and cheered Chamberlain. Cheers for Churchill came only from the Labour benches.[6]

There was no inrush of new men because Churchill set his face against any proscription of the appeasers. Both Halifax, still Foreign Secretary, and Chamberlain, now as Lord President of the Council, sat in the five-man War Cabinet at the very heart of government alongside Attlee and Greenwood from the Labour Party and Churchill himself. Outside the inner circle, of the twenty offices of Cabinet rank in the new administration, fifteen went to the Conservatives and their allies and only four to Labour and one to a Liberal. Of the 'Guilty Men', only Samuel Hoare was displaced from the Cabinet and sent off as ambassador to Madrid. The hated Conservative Chief Whip, the *bête noire* of the anti-appeasers, David

Margesson, the man who had whipped through every pro-appeasement measure of the Baldwin and Chamberlain administrations, remained in position in a joint whips office and was busy in the days after 10 May allocating junior appointments with Churchill's Private Secretary, Brendan Bracken. Another of the principal targets of *Guilty Men*, Sir Horace Wilson, regarded by many as the *éminence grise* of the Chamberlain administration, retained his powerful position as head of the Civil Service and Permanent Secretary to the Treasury. Similarly, Sir John Simon, leader of the National Liberal Party and close ally of Chamberlain – described by one historian as 'the Tweedledum of appeasement to Hoare's Tweedledee' – was allowed to become Lord Chancellor.[7] In effect, Churchill was acting in the knowledge that a majority in the House of Commons, ranged in dense ranks along the Conservative benches, was against him or only accepted him on sufferance. His failure to make a clean sweep of the old administration was an admission of political weakness within Westminster whatever the mood in the country at large. In practice, too, the exigencies of the hour, with the collapse of the Low Countries and the unfolding crisis in France, meant that this was not the time to pursue witch-hunts or to make scapegoats. Churchill loyalists like Bracken found themselves having to placate vehement anti-appeasers who had spent years in the wilderness being ostracized and ridiculed by the men who now sat alongside Churchill and whose followers still staffed the major offices of the state. Robert Boothby, irked by the reward of only a minor position in the Ministry of Food, was told, 'This is a stop-gap government formed during a whizzing crisis. Many changes will have to be made later.'[8]

But for many anti-appeasers, 'later' could not come

soon enough. As the tide of military disaster rolled over France, there were concerted moves to rid the government of the men deemed responsible for the country's plight. By early June, even as the evacuation of Dunkirk was underway, the Labour Party felt itself strong enough to launch a campaign against the 'Men of Munich' and seek the retirement of Chamberlain, Inskip, Halifax, Kingsley Wood, Butler and Simon, accompanied by a press onslaught on the 'old gang' of appeasers. On hearing of this campaign, Chamberlain appealed directly to Churchill, who in turn exhorted the Liberal and Labour leaders to put a stop to the 'heresy hunt' in the interests of national unity. They agreed, with the effect that the agitation was temporarily stilled. Churchill, whose reception in the House from Conservative members was still often half-hearted, had no reason to antagonize the Conservative majority unnecessarily nor to be distracted from the deadly serious business of securing the country's survival. According to one source, Churchill was convinced that if Chamberlain were forced out 'all his associates will go, and he [Churchill] will have to resign as jointly responsible with them for the policy of the Cabinet since the outbreak of the War' and feared that in 'internecine strife lay the German's best chance of victory'.[9]

According to some estimates it took almost two months before Churchill received something like a wholehearted endorsement from the massed Conservative benches. The occasion was the announcement of the sinking of the Vichy fleet by the Royal Navy at Oran on 4 July. One source reported that:

... something remarkable happened. The Chief Whip, Margesson, rose to his feet. Turning towards the Tory backbenchers, he waved his Order Papers in a gesture clearly conveying that they too should rise. At his signal all the Conservatives behind the Treasury bench and below the gangway . . . rose to a man and burst into enthusiastic cheering at the top of their voices.

Churchill is said to have wept; he recorded later how:

Up till this moment the Conservative Party had treated me with some reserve and it was from the Labour benches that I received the warmest welcome when I entered the House or rose on serious occasions. But now all joined in stentorian accord.[10]

Even as his popularity rose, Churchill refused to countenance a move against the appeasers, but there was continued sniping at them and continued moves by some of their most vociferous opponents to displace them. On 3 July, Clement Davies and Leo Amery were involved in holding a meeting at a Commons committee room with the ostensible purpose of 'further strengthening the present Government', deemed to be code for a purge of Chamberlain and his followers. The meeting ended in a fiasco when enough loyal Chamberlainites turned up to spoil any anti-Chamberlain resolutions. By 15 July Chamberlain could write to Hoare that 'the campaign for the elimination of the "Old Gang" and particularly your humble servant, though it has not yet come to an end, seems nevertheless to be petering out'. Although it was revived only three days later, when the 'Munich Men' were blamed for influencing the government's decision to close the Burma Road (the route along which the Chinese obtained most of their vital arms supplies) for fear of precipitating a conflict with Japan against which the Chiefs of Staff strongly advised, the irony was that this was

Churchill's decision taken against the advice of Halifax.[11] For his part, Churchill was not unhappy to have the appeasers act as a lightning conductor for some of the more unpopular decisions that had to be taken, while falling short of allowing them to be driven from office. As he opined to the *Manchester Guardian* journalist W. P. Crozier on 26 July: 'You see, after all, Chamberlain and those other people represent the Conservative Party which has a great majority in the House of Commons and they must be shown some consideration ... Chamberlain works very well with me and I can tell you this – he's no intriguer.'[12] Chamberlain was to remain in office until his retirement on 3 October due to the cancer that would kill him just over a month later.

If *Guilty Men* did not achieve its immediate objective of precipitating a purge of Chamberlainites from office during the summer of 1940, there can be little doubt that the accusations levelled at the appeasers set the tone for the interpretation of pre-war foreign policy and the period of phoney war for many years to come. In spite of the strength of pro-Chamberlainite opinion in the Commons few were prepared to protest openly at the charges levelled against them. Even the less just criticisms had to be endured unchallenged at a time when the country's dire situation seemed to vindicate virtually everything that the anti-appeasers had to say. Only when the invasion scare was well and truly past could some of the support for Chamberlain come into the open. In 1942 Tory loyalist Sir Beverley Baxter dismissed *Guilty Men* as an 'adolescent triumph' and declared his belief in the value of the Munich Agreement.[13] But while recognized as a polemical document forged at a time of great crisis, *Guilty Men* remained the most influential of the first-hand interpretations of appeasement. It portrayed appeasement as symptomatic of the whole era begun as early as 1929 under the Labour 'traitor' Ramsay MacDonald, continued under Baldwin, and brought to new depths by Chamberlain. The 'guilty men' thesis saw the policy of appeasement as a combination of calculated deception, incompetent leadership, diplomatic bungling and poor military planning. Those who passed historical judgements in the immediate post-war period tended to follow this negative lead. The evident horrors of the Nazi regime as demonstrated by the extermination camps and by the Nuremberg Trials seemed only to confirm the judgement that Hitler should have been stopped earlier rather than later. 'Appeasement' and 'Munich' were seen as synonymous with craven capitulation to force. John Wheeler-Bennett described Munich as 'a case study in the disease of political myopia which afflicted leaders and the peoples of Europe in the years between the wars'. Most influential of all was Churchill himself, who now freed of the shackles of political co-operation with the appeasers was to claim that Chamberlain had led Britain to 'the bull's eye of disaster', and demonstrate how easily the war might have been prevented by more timely action. A similar message was conveyed in the memoirs of Anthony Eden, *Facing the Dictators*, who as someone who had resigned in protest at the policy of appeasement was to present it as a misguided personal folly pursued by Chamberlain against the advice of the Cabinet and foreign office. Typical of popular perceptions at a more general level were Ronald Blythe's series of cameos of the interwar years under the pregnant title *The Age of Illusion*, which devoted its last two chapters to the Munich agreement and the fall of Chamberlain.[14]

Appeasement, alongside the failure to solve unemployment, became part of a general indictment of the governments of the 1930s, a decade represented as the 'devil's decade' or the 'locust years', an era of missed opportunities and wasted time. In this context the notion of Baldwin and Chamberlain as competent and effective leaders, of appeasement as a reasonable and justifiable policy, seemed inconceivable. Revisionism was soon abroad, however, as A. J. P. Taylor's *The Origins of the Second World War* overturned the orthodoxies by arguing that Hitler was more of an opportunist than an evil genius intent upon world domination. It was not Hitler's aggression which was the main cause of war, but rather the failure to solve German grievances with the peace settlement of 1919 and to create a genuine system of collective security. Taylor concluded that Chamberlain's policy of appeasement was logical and realistic in the circumstances, but that grave errors were made after March 1939 especially in offering a guarantee to Poland and failing to secure an Anglo-Soviet agreement which was essential to have any chance of preventing war. Hitler, Taylor argued, would have accepted a compromise over Poland and did not want war with Britain, certainly not at that point. No one was more surprised than Hitler when his bluff was finally called, the result primarily of the House of Commons forcing war on a reluctant British government.[15] Moreover, as Taylor and others pointed out, the rearmament record of governments in the 1930s was not quite as woeful as was suggested by their opponents. Although limited in scope, the decisive measures to secure air defence with radar and to provide the fighter planes which eventually won the Battle of Britain were taken by Baldwin's government. 'Cato's' attempt to exonerate the Labour Party from all blame after 1935 was a piece of special pleading. As the *New Statesman* noted, 'blame' was widely shared in the 1930s and the Left did not have an unsullied record. The 'confused attitude' of the Labour Party was cited by Taylor as late as 1937 when the impression was still being given that the Labour Party opposed rearmament and when, in fact, many of the non-trade unionist leadership were of that inclination.[16] Conversion was to come relatively late in the day for many of the Left and *Guilty Men* was, plainly, responsible not only for telescoping that process but also for producing too black-and-white a view of the complex debate over foreign policy and rearmament. Little scope was given to the major feature of the debate on all foreign policy in the period, namely the powerful surge of pacifist sentiment that was still strongly felt up to the middle of the 1930s; the memories of the appalling sacrifices of the Great War and the fear of their repetition, now compounded by the added horror of the aerial bombardment of civilian populations. When Chamberlain asked his critics what was the alternative to trying to negotiate with Hitler and bring him into the civilized practices of conventional diplomacy even at the price of humiliating concessions, the only answer appeared to be to run the risk of a war with almost unthinkable consequences.

Similarly, the scapegoating of individuals, inescapable in a piece of political polemic designed to drive the appeasers from office, jars with more considered assessments. MacDonald and Baldwin have both had more balanced evaluations than those meted out by 'Cato'. Above all, Chamberlain remains a figure of intense controversy and renewed scrutiny. For some historians, Chamberlain was not a weak-willed and ineffective leader, but a strong-willed and able politician with a clear-sighted approach to foreign policy. His aim was to avoid war, if at all possible; a war which could only weaken Britain's position in the world. To this end disputes should be settled where possible by negotiation while a prudent degree of rearmament took place. In one of the most recent studies, R. A. C. Parker has argued that though Chamberlain thought war futile he never pursued 'peace at any price'. Rather he struggled to impose his system of orderly diplomatic relations on continental Europe, even in the face of growing evidence that Hitler's appetite seemed to grow rather than be sated by concession.[17] Even when it appeared that his policy had been decisively bankrupted by Hitler's aggression against the rest of Czechoslovakia in flagrant contempt of the Munich agreement, Chamberlain's cast of mind was framed by the idea of compromise. What had begun as a policy with widespread support in the Cabinet, to secure a general settlement in Europe, became a policy pursued with obstinate, even vain self-will, against an increasing number of critics both inside and outside his party. His hopes proved deceptive and when war was declared in September 1939 he confessed that, 'Everything that I have believed in during my public life, has crashed into ruins.'[18]

But Chamberlain's double misfortune was that a man who lamented the hard lot which diverted him to foreign affairs and preparations for war when he was cut out to be a great peace-minister remained a peace-minister even in wartime. His removal from the premiership in May 1940 was to produce a much more vigorous leadership to the war effort and virtually eliminate the possibility of a compromise peace. Churchill's declaration to the Cabinet on 28 May 1940 that whatever happened at Dunkirk 'we shall fight on' was followed by the brushing aside of peace feelers from Hitler and a statement of war aims in uncompromising fashion. The Germans would have to relinquish all their gains and give 'effective guarantees by deeds, not words' that nothing of the kind would ever happen again before Britain would even condescend to negotiate. The goal was total victory. Neither the government nor the country were to deviate from these principles during the summer and autumn of 1940 nor for the duration of the war.[19] 'Cato' could rest easy, the ghost of Munich had been laid.

NOTES

1. *The Times Literary Supplement*, 20 July 1940.

2. The *Spectator*, 12 July 1940.

3. *New Statesman*, 12 July 1940.

4. A. J. P. Taylor, *English History, 1914–1945*, Harmondsworth, 1970, pp. 576–8.

5. J. Colville, *The Fringes of Power: Downing Street Diaries, 1939–1955. Vol. 1: September 1939–September 1941*, London, 1986, pp. 141–2.

6. A. J. P. Taylor, *English History*, pp. 578–9.

7. A. Roberts, *Eminent Churchillians*, London, 1994, p. 150.

8. Ibid., p. 153.

9. Ibid., p. 162; and Cecil King, *With Malice toward None: A War Diary*, London, 1970, p. 48.

10. P. Einzig, *In the Centre of Things: The Autobiography of Paul Einzig*, London, 1960, p. 221; W. S. Churchill, *The Second World War. Vol. 2: Their Finest Hour*, London, 1949, p. 211.

11. A. Roberts, *'The Holy Fox': The Life of Lord Halifax*, London, 1991, pp. 243–4. For renewed attacks, particularly on Halifax, into the autumn, see pp. 253–4.

12. A. J. P. Taylor (ed.), *Off the Record*, London, 1973, p. 175.

13. B. Evans and A. Taylor, *From Salisbury to Major: Continuity and Change in Conservative Politics*, Manchester, 1996, p. 62.

14. W. S. Churchill, *The Gathering Storm*, London, 1948, p. 31; Earl of Avon, *Facing the Dictators*, London, 1962; R. Blythe, *The Age of Illusion*, London, 1963.

15. A. J. P. Taylor, *The Origins of the Second World War*, London, 1961; see also G. Martel (ed.), *The Origins of the Second World War Reconsidered:*

The A. J. P. Taylor Debate after 25 Years, Boston, 1986; and D. C. Watt, 'Appeasement: The Rise of a Revisionist School?', *Political Quarterly*, 1965.

16. A. J. P. Taylor, *English History*, pp. 480–83, 507–8; see also P. M. Taylor, 'Appeasement: Guilty Men or Guilty Conscience', *Modern History Review*, 1989.

17. D. Marquand, *Ramsay MacDonald*, London, 1977; R. K. Middlemass and J. Barnes, *Baldwin: A Biography*, London, 1969; for a spirited defence of Chamberlain, see J. Charmley, *Chamberlain and the Lost Peace*, London, 1989. The most detailed recent study is R. A. C. Parker, *Chamberlain and Appeasement: British Policy and the Coming of the Second World War*, London, 1993.

18. For a review of 'Cato's' interpretation see S. Aster, '"Guilty Men": The Case of Neville Chamberlain', in R. Boyce and E. Robertson (eds.), *Paths to War: New Essays on the Origins of the Second World War*, London, 1989; and F. McDonough, *Neville Chamberlain, Appeasement and the British Road to War*, Manchester, 1998.

19. See A. J. P. Taylor, *English History*, pp. 595–6.

PUBLISHER'S NOTE

This edition of *Guilty Men* has been offset from the original 1940 edition. We decided that, on balance, it was preferable to keep the original print setting rather than re-setting the text, as some of the sense of polemical urgency would be lost by 'smoothing out' the book's 1940 appearance.

GUILTY MEN

PREFACE

On a spring day in 1793 a crowd of angry men burst their way through the doors of the assembly room where the French Convention was in session. A discomforted figure addressed them from the rostrum. "What do the people desire?" he asked. "The Convention has only their welfare at heart." The leader of the angry crowd replied. "The people haven't come here to be given a lot of phrases. They demand a dozen guilty men."

"The use of recriminating about the past is to enforce effective action at the present."—Mr. Winston Churchill, May 29, 1936, now Prime Minister of Britain.

CAST

Mr. Neville Chamberlain
Sir John Simon
Sir Samuel Hoare
Mr. Ramsay MacDonald
Lord Baldwin
Lord Halifax
Sir Kingsley Wood
Mr. Ernest Brown
Captain David Margesson
Sir Horace Wilson
Sir Thomas Inskip (Lord Caldecote)
Mr. Leslie Burgin
Lord Stanhope
Mr. W. S. Morrison
Sir Reginald Dorman Smith

CONTENTS

Chapter I. The Beaches of Dunkirk   *page*   7

II. Interlude Between Trains   15

III. The Duchesses were Delighted   20

IV. Enter Hitler!   26

V. The Appalling Candour of Mr. Bevin
and Mr. Baldwin   29

VI. The Navy that Sam Built   36

VII. Terrifying Power   41

VIII. Umbrella Man   45

IX. Umbrella Debate   52

X. The Golden Age   57

XI. The Grand Misalliance   64

XII. Caligula's Horse   72

XIII. Caligula's Race Horse   77

XIV. The Man with the Snow Suit   80

XV. What's there Behind the Arras?   84

CONTENTS

Chapter XVI. David   *page* 89

XVII. They Had Been Warned   94

XVIII. Portfolio Without a Minister   97

XIX. Mr. Brown, not yet Unemployed 100

XX. How To Look a Fool   103

XXI. A Friend of Mr. Chamberlain   106

XXII. An Epitaph   108

XXIII. Missing the Bus   111

XXIV. Blitzkrieg   115

CHAPTER I

THE BEACHES OF DUNKIRK

THE CAST:

The Doomed Army

A BLAZING, FEROCIOUS sun beats down on a beach which offers no shade; none except for the few precious square inches beneath the lighthouse and the pier. The sea runs out shallow for many yards from the sand and beyond the beach; between it and the town the sand dunes rise, providing at least some pretence of cover.

Mark well the dunes, the shallow sea and, most of all, the pier. The lives of three hundred thousand troops were to depend on those accidental amenities.

Dunkirk was the door at the end of a corridor no more than thirty miles wide. Inside the corridor some four hundred thousand of the picked soldiers of Britain and France waged unending battle. They were well used now to this formula of march, dig and fight. They had been doing it so long; up into the heart of Belgium, back again in perfect order when their rear was threatened, back once more when the perfidy of a King laid bare their flank.

For one moment they had sought to cut south through the enveloping German arm of steel. Alas! such a daring stroke could not be accomplished without heavy tanks and dive bombers. There was nothing else left. They glanced back over their shoulders at

7

the one speck of chance offered at the end of the corridor.

It was a ridiculous hope. Against the walls of the corridor forty German infantry divisions and eight armoured columns battered with prodigal and ceaseless fury. Even this blazing sun seemed blackened by the German planes which filled the sky. And at Dunkirk itself the most strenuous exertions of the biggest air force in the world were spent without relaxation day or night to slam the door in the face of the retreating soldiers. Berlin and London and Paris all believed that the army was doomed. No military authority would dare another prophecy. Hitler foretold "total annihilation". Winston Churchill prepared the British people for "hard and heavy tidings". M. Reynaud said that only a miracle could save them.

Here then, it seemed, was the end of the finest army which Britain had ever put in the field. Through all those days of fighting no order was given by their commanders which had not been executed. When the word was "Advance" they advanced and staked courage against superior metal in the face of machine gunning and bombing from the air. When the word was "retire", as it had so often had to be, they fell back in perfect order despite the deficiency of proper anti-tank guns to meet the onslaught, despite the continuous pitiless harrying from the air. All that courage and discipline could do they had done. They were unbeaten and unconquerable.

But all, it seemed, was of no avail. For they were now stumbling back, footsore, eyes red with weariness, sleepless for days, still pelted by all the metal which the resources of the German Reich could muster, stumbling back, aching in every limb, towards one port, already half in flames, towards one pier which one bomb could blow to oblivion. Those sands were only thirty miles from England. But they were bare, naked, inviting targets for the Nazi bomber.

Dunkirk itself was a shambles. Against it the Nazis had struck with remorseless precision. The reservoir was hit. In the hotels chartered as hospitals each wounded man was allowed only one tumbler full of water a day. There was none left for washing. Food was reduced chiefly to a ration of biscuits. So along a corridor raked by German bomb and fire, into a town crumbling in ruin and flame, on to a beach, without shade, without water, without food, without defences; to this awful extremity came the first army of Britain.

The early arrivals crowded on the beach or burrowed like rabbits amid the dunes. They gazed forlornly at the shallow waters and the pier. They were heroes; but heroism is not enough in this world of air power and seventy-ton tanks. And if the plight of those first thirty thousand was bad, what of the thousands who still fought their retreat step by step down the corridor?

That night a miracle was born. This land of Britain is rich in heroes. She had brave, daring men in her Navy and Air Force as well as in her Army. She had heroes in jerseys and sweaters and old rubber boots in all the fishing ports of Britain. That night the word went round.

In a few hours the channel was thick with barges, tugs, small coastal vessels, motor boats, lifeboats, private yachts, several hundred ships of all sizes and shapes sailing alongside British destroyers and some-times beneath the protection of British fighters. It was still a small, the slenderest of hopes.

German bombers were massing in ever increasing numbers. They machine gunned along the beach

9

which had now become as black with soldiers, in the
words of one, "as Blackpool during Wakes Week".
They hunted amid the sand dunes. They struck
hard and without discrimination in the town. They
waited in ambush for the ships. They tried their luck
at that pier. Certainly the chance was still slender.
But in all the south-east ports of Britain there was not
a man or a boy, who knew how to handle a boat who
was not prepared to give his own life to save some
unknown, valorous son of his country who had faced
without flinching the red hell of Flanders in the cause
which he knew to be his own. "I was too young to go
to France as a soldier," said a lad of eighteen who set
out with the argosy as a volunteer seaman, "but I'm
going to get damn near it."

For almost a week the epic went on. The little
ships dodged their way up the waters and hauled
over their sides the soldiers who waded waist deep,
shoulder deep to safety. The pier by some miracle
was not hit. From here the Navy did its work.

Yet every hour, except for one lucky day of fog,
the assault became hotter. More planes obscured the
sky. The machine gunners came lower and more
daring. German heavy guns coming closer down the
corridor brought the beach within range of bombardment. By the third day hopes were sinking again.
In the face of such blistering, blasting metal an awful
decision had to be taken. Embarkation could henceforth only be done at night.

With heavy, downcast heart a naval officer stepped
down the jetty to break the news. The long queues
had to squat back on the sands or return to the dunes.
They must face another twenty hours of agony.
They must have patience and strong nerves amid

perpetual din and death all about them. They had both. They were soldiers. There was no panic.

Hour after hour the work went on even though the eager seamen must now watch more carefully to slip in and out again with their human cargo. One ship was attacked six times by dive bombers across the Straits of Dover. She lay off the coast of Belgium providing an anti-aircraft barrage for other ships landing. As she pulled alongside the quay the explosions from high bombing attacks burst all around her. As she started homewards twelve more dive bombers made her their target. There was no direct hit, but an explosion burst her steampipes. She lost her way, drifted towards the sandbanks and would have stuck irrevocably had not another ship taken her in tow. Once more the vigilant dive bombers picked her out.

The Captain was nervous for his passengers. He unloaded them onto the tow ship, waved his farewell and turned to address his crew. "You have one chance," he said, "Forget the bombers and repair the steam pipes." For one and a half hours under constant fire they strove to repair the ship. At last safety was snatched from the jaws of shipwreck. She limped home to Dover. Next day she was back at Dunkirk. She was only one of a thousand. Her tale one of a million.

Thus, hungry, bandaged, thirsty, soaked in oil, salt water and blood the unbeaten Army returned to the shores of England. The first words they uttered on English soil were tributes to the seamen who had saved their lives. "God!" said one Tommy, "they were incredible. What men!" A seaman answered: "These lads are the heroes, not us," he said.

They came ashore smiling. They waved from the railway carriages. They were so proud of their saviours.

They knew they were lucky too. They had seen a comrade at their elbow struck down amid those sand dunes by a splintering piece of metal. They had blessed the good fortune of those shallow waters which enabled them to wade in and scramble aboard.

Most of all, they had sunk to their knees and thanked Heaven for that single block of concrete and wood—the pier of Dunkirk; two hundred and fifty thousand of them had come aboard from that pier. Without it half the miracle would never have happened. Certainly luck as well as heroism had saved their lives. After all the long months of training, all the terrific fighting across Belgium, all the endurance of that last, fearful week the salvation of the first Army of Britain hung through precious hours like a thread on the survival of that pier.

How was it, you may ask, that the bravest sons of Britain ever come to be placed in such jeopardy? Yes, well may you ask it. How was it, that, though the best soldiers in the world, they were driven back from Belgium? How was it that to the men along the roads of Belgium and even amid the sand dunes the German airmen seemed able to work their will as they pleased? How was it that in the last resort their safety depended not on their unmatched skill with weapons, not on their dauntless heroism, not on their unbroken discipline, but partly too on a calm sea, shallow waters and one miraculously immune pierhead?

We know the various, complicated answers. The bridges on the Meuse that were not blown up, the treacherous King of the Belgians, the mistaken notions of defensive war—all these and many more played their part. But there is another answer more truthful and more comprehensive. It was the answer stuttered out by every soldier as he stepped ashore.

Unshaven, weary, perhaps wounded he yet found time to speak the bitter truth for all the world to hear. For beneath the smiles, beneath the cheering, beneath the thanksgiving for merciful deliverance, he remembered his thirty thousand lost comrades left behind, he recalled the hell which he himself had suffered and amid his rejoicing he spoke in a voice of anger. He spoke the truth that was in him.

Here then are the right answers:

A Cornish able seaman said: "The bravest man I ever saw was an R.A.S.C. sergeant. Eight Heinkels bombed the fifty men under him who were wading ammunition to our boat. I saw several of them fall dead. The sergeant grabbed a Bren gun, stood his ground in the middle of the beach and blazed away at them. When they came back he did the same thing again and drove them off." One Bren gun and one hero against eight Heinkels. That is the right answer.

A B.E.F. infantryman said: "The finest thing I ever saw in my life was three guardsmen, the only ones left of a whole company. They stood shoulder to shoulder and plunged with their bayonets into nests of machine gunners near Dunkirk." That is the right answer. Three bayonets and three heroes against machine guns.

Another infantryman said: "We have had a few swimming lessons this last fortnight in those canals. Not much sleep, but plenty of bombs. Fifty or more Jerries would come and drop bombs. Just as we were recovering another fifty and so in relays. We longed to see our own fighters." That is the right answer. Relays of Nazi bombers against non-existent British fighters.

A Quarter-master Sergeant said: "Before embarking my men marched without sleep for nine days. They bombed us most of the time." That is the right answer. Marching men against unceasing bombers.

One infantryman said: "For the last three weeks it has been march, dig and fight. We never had a fair chance, but our time will come." That is the right answer. Unconquerable spirit against overpowering weapons. Never a fair chance.

"Three Spitfires in the sky," said another, "meant that troops were not bombarded. Why didn't we send more planes?"

Why? Why? Why?

"Give us the same equipment as the Germans," said yet another, "and we will finish them in three months." That is the right answer. Men against machines.

"Their only bitterness," wrote E. A. Montague, of the *Manchester Guardian,* and most of the other correspondents beside, "is about the lack of R.A.F. planes to defend them from the German bombers." How could they know when German planes bombed without ceasing or interference that the perhaps greatest heroes of all, the young pilots of England, were risking their lives every minute of the day against overwhelming numbers, by their skill alone were tackling four or five of the enemy, by their daring were wresting sacred m'nutes of immunity for the scarred beaches of Dunkirk. They could not know. They could not know that just as they had been pitted against superior tanks, so the last ounce of energy was being extorted from the gallant pilots to grapple with a hugely preponderating air power.

Here then in three words is the story. Flesh against steel. The flesh of heroes, but none the less, flesh. It is the story of an Army doomed *before* they took the field.

CHAPTER II

INTERLUDE BETWEEN TRAINS

THE CAST:

Ramsay MacDonald and Stanley Baldwin

THIS WAR BROKE out in 1939. But the genesis of our military misfortunes must be dated at 1929.

One sunny May morning in that year two trains stood for a few minutes close to one another in Crewe railway junction. The first train bore Prime Minister Stanley Baldwin to the North. The second one bore Socialist Leader Ramsay MacDonald *from* the North.

Both these politicians were electioneering, for a few weeks earlier Mr. Baldwin had decided to "go to the country". He was now on his way to speak in the great northern city where Mr. MacDonald had performed the previous evening. Such are the amenities of British politics that the rival protagonists hastened to greet one another and exchange opinions.

Mr. Baldwin's five years' Administration had been marked by five notable events. (i) The return to the Gold Standard, which placed the British export trade under overwhelming disabilities, thereby contributing powerfully to the attack on wages in the coal industry; (ii) The General Strike, which arose directly out of these events; (iii) An unusually eloquent debate in the House of Commons on the Prayer Book; (iv) The steady decline of British agriculture, and (v) The

BM

reduction of British air power to fifth in world rank. The Air Minister was Sir Samuel Hoare.

The unemployed stood well above a million. At the General Election Mr. Baldwin appealed to the constituencies on the slogan of "Safety First".

Mr. Ramsay MacDonald, as leader of the Parliamentary Labour Party, had formally blessed the General Strike. "Our hearts are with you," he had said, and sung the Red Flag, probably for the last time in his life. He had been a pacifist in 1914–1918 and therefore felt no anxieties now about the strength of the Air Force. Farming he did not understand, and as a Presbyterian cared nothing for the disputes over the Prayer Book. The Gold Standard which he would one day strive so earnestly to preserve, did not yet interest him. The unemployed constituted a considerable reservoir of votes, and to them he made impassioned speeches of sympathy and promise.

There was a third contestant in the electoral field of 1929. This was Lloyd George who had "won the War" by his galvanising leadership plus a prodigal expenditure of public money. Now, backed by a number of expansionist business men and inflationist economists, he proposed an energetic and grandiose programme of public works to "conquer unemployment".

Neither Mr. Baldwin nor Mr. MacDonald viewed Mr. Lloyd George with favour. The re-eruption of this incalculable figure into their orderly arena might well upset their implicit understanding of taking turn and turn about in office. Also, the fellow wanted to *do* something.

This was decisive. It was not that Lloyd George was, in the belief of either of them, about to do harm

or even do good. His offence was supremely that
he wanted to do *something*. Both Mr. Baldwin and
Mr. MacDonald had already fallen once from the
premiership by reason of doing a foolish thing;
henceforth they were resolved to sit fast and do
absolutely nothing.

Thus it came about that this May morning the Tory
Premier and the Leader of the Socialist Opposition
chatted on Crewe Station. What did they say? I
cannot remember the small talk, but this I will never
forget. As they parted Mr. MacDonald remarked,
"Well, whatever happens we shall keep out the
Welshman."

In this Mr. Baldwin and Mr. MacDonald succeeded.
They kept Lloyd George out. The national misfortune is that for the next eight years they kept themselves
in. Our country had already endured a six years'
stretch of Baldwin, MacDonald, Baldwin. It was now
to suffer a further and longer span of MacDonald, Mac-
Donald-Baldwin, and finally Baldwin-MacDonald.

First in turn, and then together they ruled Britain
for an age. They found us at the end of a great war,
wounded indeed and weary, but victorious, confident
of solving our manifold problems and capable of
doing so. MacDonald and Baldwin took over a great
empire, supreme in arms and secure in liberty. They
conducted it to the edge of national annihilation.

The unemployed remained the unemployed, except
that the million rose to two million and nearly three.
The land was denuded of 600,000 workers. The Air
Force declined from being fifth to being sixth. The
Army went unprovided, or half provided, with mechanised and motorised power. It was inadequate in
cannon, equipment and establishment.

This MacDonald-Baldwin ascendancy, so shameful and harmful to the Commonwealth, came to an end in 1937 when Earl Baldwin at last and forever resigned his seals of office. But by then we had entered deep into the region of shadow. Hitler had set up his monstrous tyranny in Germany. He had seized and fortified the Rhineland, brought in conscription, raised an Air Force which already exceeded our own, and transformed all Germany into one gigantic arsenal. The German sword was poised over Austria and Czechoslovakia.

The fearful menace of the new Nazi Imperialism had been appreciated and forcefully exposed for five years past by a few clear-eyed and courageous figures in British public life, chief of all Mr. Winston Churchill. But under MacDonald-Baldwin these warnings were derided, their authors charged with cheap adventurism or alarmism. All criticism of the régime or its own policy of ostrichism was discounted, discouraged and denounced. In the House of Commons a huge and docile majority yessed the Government through every situation. A miasma of acquiescence settled upon our parliamentary institutions and over a considerable section of the Press. Independent-minded Members went into individual opposition or, in disgust, out of public life.

When the time came, only three years ago, for MacDonald-Baldwin to wind up their firm at last and relinquish their emoluments they bequeathed to their successor, Mr. Neville Chamberlain, besides a mass of urgent problems which they had fumbled or funked, a well tested political apparatus for smudging the sharp edges of every issue and for smearing the personalities of those who raised complaint concerning it.

Thus for years Churchill was kept down—and out. He had no judgment and he wanted office! So did Amery, Lord Lloyd, Lord Wolmer. Lord Salisbury's misgivings were the fears of an old man, out of the current of information. Beaverbrook and his Grow-more-food campaigns were contemptuously smiled off. Another Press stunt! Rothermere's long propaganda for more airplanes was a House of Commons smoke-room joke. His criticism of Baldwin was, of course, a mere vendetta. When Anthony Eden and Duff Cooper could no longer tolerate the complacent betrayal of British interests they were dismissed. They could not carry corn!

The House of Commons gradually fell under the spell of this deadening influence. I shall demonstrate later exactly how the Whips' office became in time the private appanage of the Head of the Government and how the party machine of the Government parties became the instrument of his personal will. The reader will understand then just how it was possible to bring a nation to the verge of disaster.

But to grasp these facts we must patiently and clearly trace the origin and monstrous growth of this régime of little men.

CHAPTER III

THE DUCHESSES WERE DELIGHTED

THE CAST:

Ramsay MacDonald, Stanley Baldwin and John Simon

RAMSAY MACDONALD HAD hardly arrived in the Government of the United Kingdom before he took himself off on a visit to the United States.

There were two good reasons for this. One was that the Labour Party held their Annual Conference in October and he would be expected to go there and say what he had done about the unemployed. The other was that he loved the limelight and realised the Americans knew very well how to switch it on. The new Premier therefore departed for New York and Washington.

He was accorded a tumultuous triumph. His biographer has remarked that "the visit had no results of abiding importance." On his return he struck attitudes and intoned platitudes concerning the indisputable desirability of peace. In the House of Commons Mr. Baldwin warmly congratulated him, but never thought to ask him any questions as to the practical organisation of disarmament.

The MacDonald Government was pre-eminent in its practical incapacity to do anything. Industrial and agricultural distress increased sharply, and unemployment began to soar to unimagined heights. Being unable to cope with unemployment Mr. MacDonald decided to deal severely with the unemployed. He struck a great number of women off the dole. The only other positive act of his administration was to sign the London Naval Treaty which took away from Britain her freedom of design and forbade us to build the battleships we needed until 1936.

Mr. Baldwin carried on only a desultory opposition. Immediately after the General Election of 1929 Mr. MacDonald had sought out Mr. Baldwin who was still at No. 10 Downing Street and had a secret interview with him. What was discussed and agreed, has never been discovered. But in a few days' time Mr. MacDonald was hawking round the idea that the House of Commons should "constitute itself a Council of State, putting party warfare in temporary abeyance".

During this period Mr. Baldwin was having a much more serious war with Lord Beaverbrook who urged a vigorous agricultural campaign to stop the drift from the land and was trying to force his policy on the Tory Party. Against the by no means guileless newspaper baron Mr. Baldwin adopted a tactic which he later brought to perfection as a political fine art. He agreed in principle, and accepted just enough of the policy in practice to draw the teeth of the angry and earnest author who was seeking to brand him as an opponent. Nobody rejoiced more publicly at the discomfiture of Mr. Baldwin's assailant than Mr. MacDonald. He recognised in Beaverbrook another incomprehensible and uncomfortable creature with the itch to *do* something.

For his part Mr. MacDonald was thoroughly content provided he could *be* something. That something was Perpetual Prime Minister. For a long time he had been able to aspire to being Temporary Prime

Minister only by retaining the leadership of the Labour Party. He now began to look beyond that prospect and inquire if there was a more satisfactory and enduring method. He cherished the idea of becoming head of a "National" Government of all parties.

Mr. Baldwin was ready to accede. He too could think of nothing more desirable than the end of party warfare, provided he was the head of the party which had acquired effective control of the Government. Contrary to accepted belief I affirm that the National Government of MacDonald-Baldwin was planned in the spring of 1931, six months before any financial "crisis" gave urgency to the project of coalition.

There is no need to delve back into this squalid story except to note that the particular intrigue which cleared the way for the new Government appears to have been Mr. MacDonald's own. It seems that he went to his own Cabinet and told them quite untruthfully that the Tories would not support their economy measures unless there was a drastic dole cut. This the Labour Cabinet rejected, as its chief member had anticipated. He returned to the Tories and said that the Labour Cabinet rejected their proposals *in toto*. Mr. MacDonald then announced to the Tories his willingness to break with the Labour Party and form a MacDonald-Baldwin Government. The levity with which he regarded this exceptional act of treachery is revealed by his exulting remark to Lord Snowden on the day in which it was consummated. "*To-morrow every Duchess in London will be wanting to kiss me!*"

Mr. Baldwin was not less pleased with himself. He hurried his dazed partner along to a General Election which gained him 459 Tory seats while Mr. MacDonald's "National Labour" group got only a baker's dozen. It was agreed that Mr. MacDonald should continue to take the bow as Premier of the National Government, or three-ring circus of Tories, National Liberals and National Labour. The owner and ringmaster of the circus, however, was Mr. Baldwin. He permitted Mr. MacDonald to hand out some jobs to his particular followers since they were so few. Any member of the Tory Party who aspired to office was quickly made to realise that submission to Mr. Baldwin was the sole avenue of approach.

The Tory Party, indeed, was now schooled to take medicine of a kind they had never dreamed that they would have to swallow. They had to listen to Mr. MacDonald's speeches. They had to applaud them, even to try to interpret them. It was not easy.

Mr. Baldwin made no effort to restrain him. He allowed Mr. MacDonald to roam and spout all over Europe apparently without commenting on, and, quite likely, without even reading his utterances. As far as is known the relationship between these two continued on this harmonious plane right up to the end. There had been no combination like it since the Pitt-Newcastle Administration nearly two hundred years before. Pitt, like MacDonald, busied himself with foreign affairs and cared nothing for the business of domestic patronage in which the Duke of Newcastle, like Mr. Baldwin, revelled and excelled. The only obvious difference in the situation was that Pitt, by his activity, made England a great empire, while MacDonald by his oratory merely made himself a great fool.

MacDonald's folly, however, had a deeper consequence than exposing his own reputation to ridicule. At the very hour when he had been arranging the purely personal transposition of himself from Labour

23

Premier to National Premier, world-shaking and world-making events had been set in train on the far side of Asia. Japan was on the march! While the MacDonald-Baldwin bloc were piling up to a record majority on the paper ballots in the polling booths the steel-clad armies of the Mikado were trampling down the defences, and grasping the plunder, of a continent.

Neither the significance of the Japanese eruption nor of the civil commotions which were then mounting to a peak in Germany appear to have registered a discernible dent on the brain of Mr. MacDonald. He preferred to stage one more "conference triumph" at Lausanne. Mr. MacDonald was too pre-occupied with adjusting finally the Reparations of the last war to pay any heed to the danger portents of the next. He regarded Hitler, not yet in the saddle but about to vault there, and the thunderous tramping of his massed legions of ragged brownshirts as a manifestation of exuberant German youth. It was Mr. Churchill who on November 23, 1932 (mark that date!), drew to an indifferent Front Bench the first of many sombre pictures that he would present in the coming years of the gathering power and menace of a Germany that had nearly bitten through the leash. Mr. MacDonald regarded him with pity.

It would seem that Mr. Baldwin also chose to remain in ignorance. (I say "chose", because the information not only of our Secret Service but of the ordinary Intelligence of the Army, Navy and Air Force was available at all times to an energetic leading Minister. Did Mr. Baldwin avail himself of it?)

But though Mr. Baldwin's laziness seems to have inhibited him from making a study of the situation and thus arriving at the concrete reality—and the concrete enemy, his uncanny instinct for sensing "what was going on" led him to apprehend the vague shadows and monstrous shapes of the death-dealing air weapon that were beginning to form in the European sky. Speaking in the House he informed his awed hearers that "*no power on earth can protect the man in the street from being bombed. . . . The bomber will always get through*". He then declared that the only defence was offence. You had to kill the enemy's women and children more quickly than he killed yours.

He added: "*This is a question for the young men far more than it is for the old men. When the next war comes and European civilisation is wiped out, as it will be and by no force more than that force, then do not let them lay the blame upon the old men. Let them remember that they principally and they alone are responsible for the terrors that have fallen on the earth*".

Hansard records that this unbelievable piece of casuistry, coming from a leader who held the levers of power entirely in his own hands, was received in the House of Commons with "loud and prolonged cheers".

The very next Air estimates that the MacDonald-Baldwin Government introduced after this extraordinary statement were £340,000 *less* than the previous year and more than £1,000,000 *less* than the last year of the Labour Government.

CHAPTER IV

ENTER HITLER!

THE CAST:

Ramsay MacDonald, Stanley Baldwin and John Simon

ON THE 30th January, 1933, Hitler came to power in Germany. His coming fell upon Europe like the crash of a great dam in the hills.

In the Wilhelmstrasse that night two newspaper men watched the endless columns of exultant brownshirts parading by torchlight past the Chancellery. At one window of the Chancellery stood Hitler. He smiled, and saluted endlessly. At the next stood Field Marshal von Hindenburg, motionless. Turning to his friend one reporter said, "The French would be quite happy if they saw this rabble."

"No," retorted the other, "this is what the French were themselves when they stormed the Bastille. A few years later Napoleon had drilled them into the Old Guard."

It was indeed the first act of a drama as vast in scope and direful in consequence as that unfolded over Europe by the French Revolution. Before midsummer Hitler had firmly clamped his minority power (he polled about a third of the electors in the last free vote) upon the entire nation. All parties, volunteer formations, trade unions other than the Nazis, had been suppressed. The separate States of Germany had been merged into the unified Reich. Every individual critic of the Govern-

26

ment was either gaoled or scheduled for arrest. Jews, Protestants and Catholics were insulted and assaulted. An official Police Terror gripped the whole land. More. In the first hour of his first day of power, as Field Marshal Goering has since revealed, Hitler gave orders for the construction of an Air Force that should "exceed and dominate all others."

Messrs. MacDonald, Baldwin and Simon knew nothing of this last instruction. It might have been supposed that they would exercise some anxiety upon the rest of the programme of the new Spartan State and ask themselves where all this regimentation led. No such thought seems to have occurred.

The World Disarmament Conference was still in session at Geneva. It afforded Mr. MacDonald a sounding board for sonorous peroration and for his indubitable talent in persuading fifty-six delegations to agree to formulas which were acceptable to the generality because they impinged on the particular interests of none. Blind to the purposes of the criminal new Nazi war power arising in the heart of Europe, the British Premier insisted on the need to meet Germany's demands and allay her anxieties about "security". It was as though the Chief Commissioner should consult the razor gangs and weigh sympathetically their application for revolvers to protect them from the rest of the community.

It was Mr. Churchill again who injected a jet of cold sense into the situation. He said: "Thank God for the French Army." When he proceeded to charge Mr. MacDonald with leaving us more defenceless at the end of four years' office than he found us the Government claque broke out with angry denials.

Yet there were already many in the country who

had begun to feel disquietude. At the Annual meeting of the Tory Associations Lord Lloyd moved a resolution recording "its grave anxiety in regard to the inadequacy of the provisions made for Imperial defence". It was carried unanimously.

A week later Germany walked out of the League.

CHAPTER V

THE APPALLING CANDOUR OF MR. BEVIN AND MR. BALDWIN

THE CAST:

Stanley Baldwin and Samuel Hoare

I T IS OFTEN charged upon the Labour Party—by the followers of Mr. Chamberlain—that they opposed this country being armed and yet "wanted to fight Hitler".

There is just enough truth in this to make it a whopping lie.

The Party which nurtured Mr. Ramsay MacDonald was certainly permeated with severe drenchings of pacifism. Up to the arrival of Hitler on the scene, the Labour Party officially went through all the antic motions of "resisting militarism". This consisted of adopting pretty well every half-baked disarmament proposition that was drawn up, and annually voting against the Service estimates. The Fulham by-election of 1935 was nearly the final fling of this phase as far as the responsible Labour leadership was concerned. Individuals, and even groups of fools and fanatics, of course, continued to exist in the Labour Party, who were either for Peace-at-any-price or war-without-weapons. But the men who had control, who exercised the power, acted otherwise from now on.

Especially the Trade Union Congress began to realise (i) that Hitler was the implacable enemy of the trade unions, since he had reduced the German workers to the level of helots; (ii) that he was resolved to extend the bounds of his slave-state; (iii) that he could only be stopped with his own weapons. The acceptance of these precepts by the rank-and-file of Labour, constituted a genuine party revolution.

Nevertheless it was carried through in two years. As late as 1933 the Labour Party was proposing to call a General Strike in the event of the Government going to war. In 1935 the Labour Party by overwhelming vote endorsed and avowed the policy of the Government which was to challenge an Aggressor State even if it meant War.

It was not Hitler but Mussolini who brought about this reversal. For it was against the Italian Dictator that the policy of sanctions, so enthusiastically adopted by the Labour Party, were first tested.

It must be admitted by any objective student of the matter that the policy of sanctions first presented itself to the majority of the Labour Party as a non-violent method of bringing recalcitrant States to order. At worst it promised a long range economic blockade. When, therefore, Mussolini began his first great aggression against Abyssinia and Sir Samuel Hoare, the new British Foreign Secretary, stood forth at Geneva and announced that come what may Britain would fulfil her precise obligations under the Covenant, the Labour Party rapturously welcomed the forthcoming imposition of sanctions against Italy.

It was Mr. Ernest Bevin, the boss of the Transport Workers, massive and mastiff-like in appearance, shrewd and penetrating in intelligence, who put the picture into sharp perspective.

The Dome at Brighton was packed with delegates at the Labour Party Conference on October 1, 1935. They gave an enthusiastic welcome to their leader, the benign be-whiskered Victorian veteran Pacifist, George Lansbury, when he stood up to address them. George Lansbury was a sincere sentimentalist with an idea a good deal more clearly fixed in his brain than most of his 'realist' detractors. He believed in passive resistance. Under no condition would he subscribe to coercion if it involved blood letting.

Lansbury was well aware of the perils of the path the Labour Executive had embarked on when they sponsored the motion in favour of supporting sanctions, but the weakness of his position was that he had not opposed it emphatically enough during the discussions of the Executive when this policy was taking shape. Now he realised it and he spoke affectionately and sorrowfully of saying farewell to his old colleagues and followers, a statement which called forth loud cries of NO! from the body of the assembly but no dissent from the platform. Speaking with genuine passion, the old man delivered himself of his last plea for non-violence. "Those who take the sword shall perish by the sword! Vengeance is *mine* saith the Lord. *I* will repay."

A profound emotion surged over the gathering. Ernest Bevin rolled to the tribune. He also understood the perils of sanctions. He also had faced them in his long, solitary communings with himself. He had discussed them thoroughly in all their aspects with his colleagues before publicly subscribing to them, and he had bitterly resented it when Lansbury, without consultation, had gone off and expressed *his* anxieties to a Press Association reporter. Now he resolved to deal finally with the issue.

"This conference," Bevin boomed, "ought to be influenced neither by sentiment nor personal attachment, We ought not to be put in the position of watching

CM

Lansbury cart his conscience round from conference to conference asking to be told what to do with it."

At these brutal words there was a spontaneous movement of indignation among the delegates and loud protests. Bevin stood like a granite pier in a tempestuous sea. Above the storm he roared "Do unto others . . .! Lansbury should have faced the issue long ago. But instead of coming back to us in executive Council and saying he was in difficulties, he got on to a 'P.A.' reporter—on a Sunday. . . ."

At this gibe against Lansbury's well known Sabbath observance the Conference rose again. There was a roar of "Shame! Withdraw!" Bevin crashed through the barrage, "The Monroe doctrine is sanctions. And it is good. It is America's choice. It keeps peace in the Continent of America. Pacifism is what China chose. Look at China!" He then expounded to the Conference that sanctions might mean war and he was ready if it came. Lansbury sat there with the tears running down his face. His plea was shattered and his heart was broken.

Afterwards someone said to Bevin, "You were rough on the old boy." He replied, "Lansbury has been going about dressed up in saint's clothes for years waiting for martyrdom. I set fire to the faggots."

This was the appalling candour of Ernest Bevin in 1935. Henceforth the Labour Party was officially pledged to armaments every whit as much as the Government. Unhappily, it was not until 1940 that Ernest Bevin became part of the Government.

Now we come to the appalling candour of Mr. Baldwin. How did "Honest Stanley" Baldwin handle the question of armaments before the eyes of his people?

We must turn back the pages for a few months. Facing a new onslaught in the House of Commons by Mr. Winston Churchill, Mr. Baldwin had given this specific undertaking:

"This Government will see to it that in air strength and air power this country shall no longer be in a position inferior to any country within striking distance of our shores."

The date was March 8, 1934. A few days later Lord Londonderry, the Air Minister, in the House of Lords dismissed as impracticable the idea that a Supreme Minister of Defence be made responsible for the three Services. Everything was declared to be going forward with expedition and efficiency under the existing arrangements.

The months passed. In the Autumn Churchill returned to the assault. He categorically asserted:

(i) That Germany had a secret and illegal air force already nearly equal to the strength of Britain. (Germany was at this time still prohibited by the Peace Treaty from having any Air Force);

(ii) That within twelve months Germany's Air Force would be as strong as ours;

(iii) That in two years Germany would be fifty per cent stronger in the air than Britain;

(iv) That in three years they would be nearly double our strength.

Mr. Churchill challenged the Government to deny his propositions.

Mr. Baldwin could not agree that there was any "immediate menace" or even "emergency". He flatly contradicted Churchill's figures.

"It is not the case that Germany is rapidly approaching equality with us. Her real strength is not fifty per cent of our strength in Europe to-day."

33

The date was November 28, 1934.

In March, 1935, Hitler brought in conscription for Germany. He also announced that Germany had an Air Force and that it was already equal to Britain's. At the beginning of May, Mr. Baldwin had to eat his words of November. With that characteristic gesture of manfully taking the blame for what was in fact his fault, Mr. Baldwin proclaimed:

"I only want to repeat that, whatever responsibility there may be—and we are perfectly ready to meet criticism—that responsibility is not that of any single Minister; it is the responsibility of the Government as a whole, and we are all responsible, and we are all to blame."

He ended the month of May by addressing his followers at the Albert Hall. He assured them:

"No Government in this country could live a day that was content to have an Air Force of any inferiority to any country within striking distance of our shores."

This seemed a firm enough assurance of Air security to those who had entertained such grave apprehensions as to our strength. Quite soon, however, another set of considerations began to impinge on Mr. Baldwin's mind. A General Election was in the offing and the very large "Peace Vote" could not be ignored. A few days before polling Mr. Baldwin brought himself to offer this explanation—and this pledge—to the Peace Society:

"Do not fear or misunderstand when the Government say they are looking to our defences. I give you my word that there will be no great armaments."

34

The date was October 31, 1935.

So Mr. Baldwin, who, by the way, had now become Prime Minister again by shuffling posts with Mr. MacDonald who had become entirely incoherent, went to his election promising both an Air Force equal to Hitler's and at the same time "no great armaments".

Mr. Baldwin found no inconsistency in this (nor, alas, did the electors), for he was at the same time promising to prevent Mussolini making war on Abyssinia and yet not to involve us in war ourselves.

One year later "Honest" Baldwin declared to the House of Commons that he would "speak with appalling candour." He then delivered himself of this extraordinary pronouncement.

"From 1933, I myself and my friends were all getting very worried about what was happening in Europe. . . .

"I asked myself what chance was there of this country, where the feeling expressed at Fulham was so common, being so changed in the next year or two that the country would give a mandate for re-armament?

"Now, supposing I had gone to the country and had said 'Germany is rearming; we must rearm'. Does any one think that this pacific democracy of ours would have rallied to that cry? Not at that moment.

"I cannot think of any change which would have made the loss of the election, from my point of view, more certain."

"We won the election by a large majority," he continued.

The most extraordinary thing of all is that the Government benches swallowed this entire dirty dish without a tremor or a protest.

Indeed, with his colleagues and followers, Mr. Baldwin's stock stood higher than ever.

CHAPTER VI

THE NAVY THAT SAM BUILT

THE CAST:

*Sir Samuel Hoare, Herr von Ribbentrop, and
Signor Mussolini*

SIR SAMUEL HOARE was Mr. Baldwin's Air
Minister in 1923, a post to which he was re-appointed,
for the third time, by Mr. Neville Chamberlain in 1940.

In the meantime, Sir Samuel had been Secretary
for India, Foreign Secretary, First Lord of theAdmiralty,
Home Secretary, and Lord Privy Seal. He is now
Ambassador to Spain. This period has covered nine
different Governments, together with innumerable
re-shuffles. It is a tribute to Sir Samuel's astonishing
capacity to endure the arrows of outrageous fortune
that he could survive seventeen years of political battle
and still emerge at the very same door wherein he
entered. Like the Abbé Sieyes who was asked what he
had done in the Great French Revolution Sir Samuel
could faithfully reply "I kept alive".

In June, 1935, Sir Samuel happened to be Foreign
Minister. He thought it would be a great stroke to
make a naval treaty with Germany. That is, Sir Samuel
thought it would be a great stroke to accede to Germany's demand that a naval treaty should be made.
The power of initiating any move had long since
departed from the Government of Britain.

Very quickly the deal was done. Von Ribbentrop

saw to that. The baggy-eyed Champagne tout was Hitler's new Ambassador-at-large. He completely pushed into the background Herr von Hoesch, the German Ambassador to London and Baron von Neurath, the German Foreign Minister, both of whom he meant to supersede. It was von Ribbentrop who closed the bargain with Sir Samuel Hoare.

The treaty was signed on June 18, the day of Waterloo. It specified that Germany should be permitted thirty-five per cent of the total naval tonnage of the British Empire. In the submarine class she was to be allowed up to forty-five per cent. Germany pledged herself never to engage in "unrestricted submarine warfare".

This treaty was rapturously greeted in the British press, Right, Left and Centre. The only dissidents were at the very extremities of this wide front, the *Morning Post* and the *Daily Worker*. In Parliament it was welcomed—except by Mr. Churchill, Lord Lloyd and Admiral Keyes. These critics pointed out that if the Nazis were insisting on forty-five per cent instead of 35 per cent in the special category of submarines the supposition was that they proposed to make effective use of this arm in war. If this were true it was inconceivable that the Nazis would sit still and let a British blockade starve them again without once more resorting to "unrestricted submarine warfare". Churchill warned "such a view must constitute the acme of gullibility". The Government and the House of Commons preferred von Ribbentrop's assurances.

Later, when the real implications of this treaty became plain and it was commonly said "Sam Hoare is the creator of the German Navy" the Government's friends denied it and put out an ingenuous explanation. They said that in fact the German Navy had already been built up to thirty-five per cent of the British strength and that Sir Samuel Hoare was simply "recognising facts".

If this were true the Government had a still more serious charge to face. Why didn't they know about the German building? After all, you cannot build a battleship in a boat-house. Did nobody know, and report, these immense constructions? Did the Secret Service, did the Naval Intelligence fail in its duty?

The alternatives are that either the Secret Service *did* know and *did* report, and that somewhere between their department and the Minister somebody watered down the facts; or else the Ministers deliberately lied to the House of Commons and the Nation. I should be unwilling to accept this last possibility.

The Anglo-German Naval proposals, which, of course, assured naval predominance to Germany in the Baltic, were not communicated to the Soviet Government. The Russians were merely informed of the terms when they had been settled. Four years later Sir Samuel Hoare spoke in terms of trembling indignation when the Russians settled their pact with the Germans over Poland without notifying the British Government until the deal was closed.

It did not even occur to this clever fumbler to tell the French. Only a few months earlier Britain had joined with France and Italy to condemn Germany's unilateral breach of the Treaty of Versailles in introducing conscription. Sir Samuel was now invoking the sacred name of the Covenant of the League of Nations (the Guardian of the Treaties) against the projected aggression of the Italians in Abyssinia. Yet at this precise hour he chose to condone the German defiance of Versailles in building herself a navy. He proposed to sanctify treaty-breaking by sealing a new treaty.

France was furious. Italy mocked. Russia withdrew

into deeper suspicions. Germany rejoiced. She had gained the blessing of one of the principal signatories of the Versailles Treaty for an act which abolished some of its principal clauses. She had acquired the legal right to build warships up to the point she needed —with the prospect of building beyond that point the moment it suited her to denounce her latest undertaking. This of course is what happened. In April 1939 Hitler abrogated the Anglo-German Naval Treaty.

Meantime, Von Ribbentrop's stock soared in Berlin. He had done so well in dishing Sir Samuel Hoare that it was resolved to accredit him as official ambassador to Britain, where he would have the opportunity of dishing the entire Government.

As Foreign Secretary Sir Samuel Hoare passed from experience to experience, like Boccaccio's virgin, without discernible effect upon his condition.

Having seriously alarmed the French by showing them that Britain would act alone when it suited her he now engaged in conflict with the Italians over Abyssinia, requiring the French to support him to uphold the sanctity of treaties. This was rather too much for M. Laval.

In any event M. Laval had some months earlier at the Stresa Conference of Britain, France and Italy, indicated to Mussolini that he proposed to cock a blind eye to any troubles that might arise over Abyssinia.

This was not a high moral engagement but there is this much to be said for M. Laval. He did indicate his intentions to his British ally at the time. The British representatives (they were MacDonald and Simon) chose to ignore this matter on the principle that what you don't know about you won't worry about.

The end of this pitiable story is quickly reached. Believing Britain meant business the Abyssinians stood up to the Italians. Believing that Mussolini would quit, the British Government sent the fleet to the Mediterranean and applied economic sanctions to Italy. When Mussolini indicated that he would not regard this as war unless we made the sanctions serious the British Government refrained from making them serious.

Mussolini went ahead. Halfway through his conquest Sir Samuel Hoare proposed that he should be confirmed in his gains to date and the war called off. Mr. Baldwin agreed. But when public uproar broke out in Britain he changed his mind and changed his Foreign Secretary. Sir Samuel retired in a flood of tears. Lloyd George said he made a speech like a "scivvy asking for a reference". But really Sir Samuel did not need to "ask for a reference". He had something more valuable— an understanding with his boss. Six months later he was re-employed as First Lord of the Admiralty.

As for Mr. Baldwin, when he was caught with the cards he simply produced another ace. "My lips are sealed," he cried. "But if these troubles were over I would make such a case that no man would go into the lobby against me."

In fact, Mr. Baldwin and Sir Samuel Hoare had tried to bluff Mussolini, had found their bluff called, and had then sought to make a sharp deal with him but had been prevented by onlookers.

But why had their bluff been called?

If Mr. Baldwin's mystic words meant anything they could only have meant this: that he and his colleagues had let their country's defences fall into such disrepair that, being challenged, they dare not risk a war even against a second rate bully like Mussolini.

CHAPTER VII

TERRIFYING POWER

THE CAST:

Mr. Chamberlain

A SIGH OF relief was audible in the country as Mr. Chamberlain succeeded Lord Baldwin in the Premiership in the Spring of 1937. The nation believed that something better must come since there could be nothing worse. For the apple-blossom of Bewdley was to be substituted the hardware of Birmingham. Whatever else was lost by this exchange, the nation's defences could surely benefit.

This is no place to give an account of Mr. Chamberlain's performance in foreign affairs. I intend only to tabulate his promises regarding the country's preparations for war should the foreign policy fail.

Mr. Chamberlain had always employed a stronger accent than his leader; he had supported to the hilt all the Government's dealings with foreign powers. He had made the necessity of supporting Abyssinia a key point in his election address of 1935. He had approved the Hoare-Laval deal with the same enthusiasm that Mr. Baldwin himself had shown. He agreed to jettison that deal and revert to the sanctions policy when the nation unmistakably expressed its abhorrence at our desertion of Haile Selassie. Finally when Haile Selassie's cause was hopelessly lost it was Mr. Chamberlain who emphatically voiced the Cabinet's opinion that further sanctions were "Midsummer Madness" and should be forthwith wound up.

Nevertheless, through all these shifts and changes, for which he was not primarily responsible, Mr. Chamberlain held firmly to one project—the urgent need for British rearmament.

"If we are to make our contribution to that general sense of security in Europe," he said in January 1935, "we must at all events be sufficiently armed to be able to do so."

Eleven months later, on the night before the General Election of 1935, he admitted that this sufficiency in arms had by no means been achieved. "The Government has been conscious," he said, "that their hands have been weakened by the knowledge of other countries that Britain was not strong enough either at sea or on land to make her words good if trouble were to come."

Another eight months passed and he was still dissatisfied with the nation's state of preparedness. "No one looking around the three continents of Europe, Asia and Africa," he said, "can doubt that if we are to play our part in preserving the peace of these great regions, if indeed we are to maintain our own imperial interests and vital lines of imperial communication, it is absolutely necessary that we should rehabilitate our armed forces without delay."

Presumably the necessity was still as great ten months later when Mr. Chamberlain stepped up into Mr. Baldwin's shoes equipped now with almighty power to ensure that nothing should be left undone in this supreme task.

Yet late in that Autumn of 1937, Mr. Chamberlain was still dissatisfied with the progress of the nation's defences, despite the months of preparation and despite his warning years before that the need was imperative. A war had started in Spain and Hitler had torn up a few more clauses in the Treaty of Versailles. Those developments should surely have stressed the urgency. Yet speaking of the rearmament plan Mr. Chamberlain declared: "I must frankly admit that progress is not yet as fast as I should like, but it soon will be." A great amount of preparatory work still remained to be done. "I am glad to say," he continued, "that this preparatory stage is now practically completed and that production has begun in earnest." *In earnest*. That was surely a promise of better things.

December 1937 found Mr. Chamberlain growing in confidence in the nation's strength. It was just as well. Another war was blazing in the Far East and the Spanish furnace was getting hotter. As he packed Lord Halifax off to see Hitler, the Premier gave his expression to this new spirit. "The country is strong," he said. "She is getting stronger every day. Our strength makes it easier for us to appeal to others to join us in applying our common sense to these problems."

How that common sense was to be applied was speedily shown in the New Year. A break was made with Mr. Eden who required that the old agreements with Mussolini should be carried out before new ones were made; Mr. Chamberlain preferred to accept Mussolini's assurances of "perfect good faith". A stern rebuke was issued to those cantankerous persons who complained that Herr Hitler had delivered an ultimatum to Herr Schuschnigg on February 12th. A comprehensive indictment was made against the Opposition who would not accept these blithe assurances. "They are living in an unreal world," said Mr. Chamberlain in one notable debate.

43

It is true that neither of these events turned out quite as Mr. Chamberlain had prophesied. Mussolini's troops stayed in Spain. Hitler's troops invaded Austria. Mr. Chamberlain was not abashed. He promised more appeasement, and if that did not quite satisfy his critics he promised more rearmament. Now at last he was fully satisfied with that programme.

In March 1938 he said: "The almost terrifying power that Britain is building up has a sobering effect on the opinion of the world."

The sobering effect did not persist six months later when Hitler massed his troops on the borders of Czecho-Slovakia and when Mr. Chamberlain himself went to Berchtesgaden to accept a Hitler ultimatum. Hitler at least was not terrified by our power.

Yet it is necessary to fix the dates squarely in the memory. A year after he had assumed the Premiership Mr. Chamberlain believed that the strength of our armaments was such that it was "terrifying" to foreign powers. That was six months before Munich, eighteen months before the outbreak of this war, eighteen months before the Chief of our Imperial General Staff admitted that he "trembled to think" what would have happened if Hitler had broken through on the Western Front; two years before Hitler did in fact break through on the Western Front with superior tanks and overwhelming numbers of airplanes.

CHAPTER VIII

UMBRELLA MAN

THE CAST:

All the Characters

ON A HOT summer afternoon several hundred years ago a Balkan peasant arose from the stone he was squatting upon and began to dance.

Quickly the villagers ran to the spot. They gaped at the remarkable spectacle of a man twirling and gyrating all by himself in the sunlight. They giggled.

But presently the man's dance became more frantic. His eyes began to stare. Foam drooled from his lips and nostrils.

The peasants watching him began to tap their feet in sympathy. Soon they began to dance too.

They streamed across the countryside in a frenzy, dancing all the way. Wherever they went, others joined the dance.

The dance mania spread all over Europe, from country to country. Women gashed themselves with knives as they capered. Men dashed their heads against walls. When the madness spread across the sea to England, over five hundred deaths were reported as a result of the dancing. The hysteria did not depart from Europe for many months. . . .

At about half past four on a warm autumn afternoon September 28, 1938, an exhibition of hysteria, the result of which was also destined to spread over the

45

whole face of Europe, took place in the British House
of Commons.

Honourable and right honourable gentlemen yelled
and screamed like football fans. Three Tory members
put their arms around each other's necks and hopped
up and down in the lobby exclaiming, "Thank God for
the Prime Minister, thank God for the Prime Minister."

Sixteen men and two women as they walked out of
the Chamber, were sobbing and crying with emotion.

The cause of this outburst was physical. For many
days M.P.s had felt that war with Germany over the
issue of the Sudeten Deutsch minority in Czechoslovakia
was inevitable.

Gas masks had been distributed to all the citizens
(except small children. The Government had made no
provision for them). Trenches were being dug in the
turf of the London parks.

Parliament had met with almost every member of it
oppressed by fear. They believed that the Prime
Minister was going to announce that we were entering
into war with Germany.

Mr. Chamberlain, in a sentence removed that fear.
While he was giving his account of events a message
from the Foreign Office was passed along the Front
Bench and handed to him.

Having glanced at it, Mr. Chamberlain's cheeks
changed colour. A healthy brown tinge appeared on his
ashen countenance. He informed the House of Commons
that he was going to Munich next day to meet Hitler.
Then the dance of delight began.

The events, which led up to this scene must be briefly
set out in order to complete the picture.

For a long time German propaganda had been
directed to fomenting discontent and violence among

the German minority inside Czechoslovakia. Hitler had constantly said that he would not tolerate such a situation and that the Sudeten Germans must be restored to the Reich.

In June, 1938, the Nazi threats became violent. Mr. Chamberlain thereupon sent Lord Runciman to Czechoslovakia to attempt to negotiate a compromise between the Czechs and the Germans.

Early in August, Germany began to mobilise, and Ribbentrop told the British ambassador in Berlin that his country was determined to find a solution of the problem by the autumn.

All through August, the situation became worse. Lord Runciman was browbeating the Czechs and urging them to be more accommodating. German demands were increasing and were set out in ever more menacing terms.

On September 12, Hitler made a speech at Nuremberg saying that the German army was mobilised on the Czech frontier and that he supported the Sudeten Germans in their demand for freedom.

By the evening of September 14 a German invasion of Czechoslovakia seemed certain within a few hours.

At this point Mr. Chamberlain decided to put into effect a plan which as far back as May, 1938, he had been discussing with his friends. This plan was suggested by Sir Horace Wilson, at that time Industrial Adviser to the Government, who, though in his capacity as Civil Servant was concealed from public gaze behind the arras (like Polonius in Hamlet), just the same played a major rôle in these events.

The plan was that Mr. Chamberlain should make a personal visit to Hitler and try to do a deal with him. Accordingly, the British Prime Minister sent an urgent

DM

47

message to the German Führer asking if that gentleman would be at home on the following afternoon.

On September 15, Mr. Chamberlain flew off to Berchtesgaden. Hitler told Mr. Chamberlain with great candour that if the Sudeten Germans were not at once returned to the Reich, he was ready to risk world war on their behalf.

Mr. Chamberlain replied that in that case he had been wasting his time and that he could not understand why Hitler, contemplating an immediate invasion of Czechoslovakia, had allowed him to travel all that way. Hitler answered that if the British Government would give him an assurance that the principle of self-determination for the Sudeten Germans would be accepted, he would be quite ready to discuss methods of carrying it out. Otherwise it was useless to continue the conversation.

Next day the British Minister flew home. The British Government decided, in consultation with the French, to force the Czech Government to agree to cede all territory with more than 50 per cent Sudeten German inhabitants to Germany. With difficulty, the Czechs were persuaded to agree to this plan. The bribe offered to them was that the British and French Governments undertook to guarantee the future boundaries of the now truncated Czechoslovakia against aggression.

The method to be adopted for the transfer of territory to Germany was that an international body should be set up to deal with the adjustment of frontiers.

Mr. Chamberlain sighed with satisfaction when this distasteful scheme had, by the united efforts of himself and the French Premier, been crammed down the reluctant gullet of the Czech rulers and eventually, with many a groan and retch, swallowed into their stomachs.

The Prime Minister perhaps felt the same delight as a farmer who has completed the job of drenching an obdurate horse for the good of its health, when he climbed once more into his airplane on the morning of September 22 and flew to Godesberg.

There Hitler told him bluntly that although he perceived the British Government had advanced far beyond the point of agreeing to the principle of self-determination for the Sudeten Germans he had unfortunately changed his mind. The proposals which Mr. Chamberlain brought were no longer acceptable. The procedure suggested was too slow.

Hitler demanded in fact that almost every part of Czechoslovakia where a German could be found should be handed over at once to the Reich. The whole affair was to be completed by October 1. There was to be no more delay or negotiation.

Hitler also said that this was the last of his territorial ambitions in Europe, that he wanted to be friends with England, and that if the Sudeten question could be got out of the way, he would like to resume conversations with the British Premier.

Mr. Chamberlain came home once more. He passed on Hitler's proposals to the Czechs who refused them, and completed full mobilisation of their army.

On September 26 Sir Horace Wilson was sent to Berlin to see Hitler and to propose that there should be an immediate discussion between German and Czech representatives in the presence of British representatives. Hitler refused. He said there was to be no more procrastination.

The following morning the British Fleet was mobilised. Mr. Chamberlain sent one more message to Hitler saying that he would like to see him again as he was convinced agreement could be reached in a week.

Next day the invitation to Munich was passed to Mr. Chamberlain as he was giving Parliament his account of events, and the remarkable exhibition of delight which has already been described took place on the benches of Westminster.

* * * * *

Next morning the Ministers who had risen early and motored to Heston to cheer the departing Premier as he stepped into the airplane, saw on the tape when they returned to their office that Mr. Chamberlain was already over German territory.

The Prime Minister at Munich in effect agreed with Hitler that his Godesberg demands should be granted. The Czechs were told that if they objected to the deal they would fight against Germany alone. They surrendered their objections.

The modifications between the proposition Mr. Chamberlain rejected at Godesberg and accepted at Munich were so slight that Mr. Churchill described the position in these terms: "At Berchtesgaden £1 was demanded at pistol point. When it was given (at Godesberg) £2 were demanded at pistol point. Finally (at Munich) the dictator consented to take £1 17s. 6d. and the rest in promises of goodwill for the future."

The goodwill guarantee for the future was contained in a piece of paper which Mr. Chamberlain fluttered in his hand as he descended from his airplane on the return from Munich. This document was signed by both the German Führer and the British Premier.

It declared that Britain and Germany did not want to fight each other any more and would take consultation with each other on points of difficulty which might arise.

So, having cheered the British Premier once more for his efforts, M.P.s scattered to their homes for a week-end of joy and relaxation.

On that Sunday, October 2, 1938, the German tanks and troops advanced unopposed across the Czech frontier to take over their new territory (which included, intact, all the fortifications and gun emplacements the Czechs had bled themselves to erect on this German frontier during the previous five years).

On that same Sunday this prayer was ordered to be read in all Catholic Churches by the Roman Catholic Cardinal, Primate of Bohemia.

"The land of St. Wenceslas has just been invaded by foreign armies and the thousand-year-old frontier has been violated. This sacrifice has been imposed on the nation of St. Wenceslas by our ally, France, and our friend, Britain. The Primate of the ancient Kingdom of Bohemia is praying to God Almighty that the peace efforts prompting this terrible sacrifice will be crowned by permanent success and, should they not, he is praying to the Almighty to forgive all those who impose this injustice on the people of Czechoslovakia."

· · · · ·

In the Protestant churches of Czechoslovakia the same prayer was offered with the substitution of the name "John Huss" for "Saint Wenceslas".

CHAPTER IX

UMBRELLA DEBATE

THE CAST:

*Mr. Chamberlain, Sir Thomas Inskip, and
Sir John Simon*

FOR THE FIRST two days of the next week Parliament discussed the decision reached by the Premier at Munich. Throughout this debate the mood of hysterical approbation was prolonged. M.P.s vied with each other in their exertions to lick the hand of the Premier—or even touch the hem of his garment in debate.

Mr. Victor Raikes, the Tory Member for S.E. Essex, gave expression to the sentiment of at least five out of six M.P.s of all parties at that moment when he exclaimed, "There should be full appreciation of the fact that our leader will go down to history as the greatest European statesman of this or any other time."

It is true that the Parliamentary proceedings began with an unhappy episode. Mr. Duff Cooper rose and explained to the House of Commons that he so utterly disapproved of the Munich deal that he had resigned from the Government. (Mr. Duff Cooper, as First Lord of the Admiralty, had been responsible for mobilising the British Fleet while Sir Horace Wilson was in Berlin. Mr. Duff Cooper appeared to think, probably correctly, that his deed rather than the words of Sir

Horace had influenced Hitler's mood when he invited Mr. Chamberlain to Munich.)

Mr. Duff Cooper performed an act of high political courage in resigning when he did. It is an easy thing to leave a Government which is struggling in the trough of the waves, pursuing a policy unpopular with the public (vide Mr. Eden's resignation on the grounds that Mr. Chamberlain should not trust Mussolini). It is far harder to leap overboard from the ship of state when it is at the crest, curling through the waters, in the sunshine of public approbation.

In his personal explanation to the House of Commons Mr. Duff Cooper remarked, "When we were discussing the Godesberg ultimatum, I said that if I were a party to persuading or even to suggesting to the Czechoslovak Government that they should accept that ultimatum, I should never be able to hold up my head again . . . I have ruined, perhaps, my political career. But that is a little matter. I have retained something which is to me of great value—I can still walk about the world with my head erect."

Mr. Duff Cooper's resignation was brushed aside by Mr. Chamberlain, who gave an account of his dealings with Hitler. He justified his actions by saying that under the new system of guarantees the new Czechoslovakia would find a greater security than she had ever enjoyed in the past. In addition he announced that the British Government were going to make a present of £30,000,000 to the Czechs to help them overcome the economic difficulties they would be bound to meet on account of their loss of valuable territory.

Outside in the Smoke Room, while the debate was going on, an incident occurred which was never reported in the newspapers. One of Duff Cooper's friends remarked, "The world is changing. Values have improved. Two thousand years ago a man could reckon on receiving 30 pieces of silver if he went in for a betrayal. Now a nation has to pay out 30 million pieces of gold if it goes in for a betrayal."

This M.P. was at once knocked down by a fellow-legislator. He went home in a taxi with a bloody nose.

Inside the Chamber, in spite of the immense support which the Premier was receiving from end to end of the land, some criticism was offered him.

Mr. Attlee, Sir Archibald Sinclair, Mr. Eden and Mr. Churchill all risked and incurred odium by saying that this country had suffered unmitigated defeat at Munich.

But the extraordinary feature of the Munich debate was this. Although the Prime Minister, on his return from the last visit to Germany, had told the listening earth as he waved his little piece of paper in the air, "This is Peace in our time," the main discussion in Parliament became directed to the issue of rearmament.

On this point, the whole House was united. Mr. Churchill marched in step with Mr. Chamberlain. Mr. Attlee and Mr. Duff Cooper and the whole crowd of them lined up with the Government. There was a unanimous and spontaneous viewpoint, expressed the most vigorously by those men who voiced loudly the opinion that Peace in our Time was a reality, and not an old man's dream, that Britain must now rearm day and night, night and day.

Mr. Chamberlain said in the Munich debate, "We must renew our determination to fill up the deficiencies that yet remain in our armaments."

Sir Samuel Hoare declared, "We are perfectly prepared to have our record examined as to our defence preparations. . . . We are determined to fill up the gaps which have shown themselves in our defensive armaments."

Mr. Burgin remarked, "Because we believe it is a contribution to peace we will examine and make good gaps and deficiencies in our own system of active and passive defence."

(After this speech the late Capt. Sir Sidney Herbert was growled and shouted at because he arose and said, "We have talked long enough about 'the years which the locusts have eaten'. I was led to suppose that the locusts had stopped nibbling about two years ago, but I can hear their little jowls creaking yet under the Front Bench." Sir Sidney at this point concentrated his gaze on Sir Kingsley Wood.)

Sir Thomas Inskip, who deserves and will receive detailed attention in these pages, assured the House of Commons, "The essential war materials, including a number of rare metals, have been accumulated in stock sufficient to carry us through a long war."

Sir John Simon told the House that the Government had seen shortcomings in their defensive arrangements and would hasten to put them right.

In fact, over the question of rearmament absolute unanimity was achieved at the Munich debate. Even the minority members who opposed the Munich settlement were soothed and silenced by the expressed resolve of the Government now to set about the rearmament of Britain with energy.

So strong was this emotion that the Tory Central office cashed in on it as a piece of political propaganda. They put around in the constituencies of the few obdurate anti-Munich Tory M.P.s that the Prime Minister had made his bargain with Hitler not from choice but from necessity. Britain was not ready to fight. But she was going to get ready now.

This propaganda had success. Everyone, even Mr. Chamberlain's bitter critics, believed that we were about to rearm on a scale which would amaze the world.

So the nation was comforted.

CHAPTER X

THE GOLDEN AGE

Messrs. Chamberlain and Hitler and the Geese

WHEN MR. CHAMBERLAIN stepped out of his airplane on the return from Munich, he had said, "This means Peace in our time."

After he got back to Downing Street he shouted from the window, "I bring you Peace with honour." He also remarked, "Out of this nettle, danger, we pluck this flower, safety."

Nobody can accuse Mr. Chamberlain of being a wilful liar. He said those things because he believed them. He was absolutely satisfied that when Hitler signed that little piece of paper, the heart of a man who had built up his régime by treachery, lies and deception, had changed.

Chamberlain trusted Hitler. "I have no hesitation in saying," he said in Parliament, "after the personal contact I established with Herr Hitler that I believe he means what he says" (in the reassuring statements he had made to Chamberlain).

At a dinner party shortly after Munich, the British Prime Minister found himself sitting near to a politician who had opposed the settlement. A discussion arose between the two men and was conducted in most friendly terms.

The Premier's opponent asked how any trust

could reasonably be placed in Hitler's word. He
pointed out that as long ago as 1933 Hitler said in
the Reichstag, "The German people have no thought
of invading any country." In 1934 he said, "After the
Saar question is settled, the German Government
is ready to accept not only the letter but also the
spirit of the Locarno Pact." In May 1935, in the
Reichstag, the German Führer said, "Germany
neither intends nor wishes to interfere in the internal
affairs of Austria, to annex Austria or to conclude
an Anschluss." In March 1936 he affirmed, "We
have no territorial demands to make in Europe."

In February 1938 he reaffirmed his recognition
of Austrian sovereignty already expressed in the
Austro-German agreement of July 1936.

In March 1938 he gave assurances that Germany
had no hostile intention against Czechoslovakia.

Having recited all these broken pledges, this fellow
guest turned towards Mr. Chamberlain at the dinner
table and asked, "Prime Minister, in the face of all
this, remembering all these things, do you not feel
a twinge of doubt about Hitler's promises?"

Mr. Chamberlain replied with complete gravity,
"Ah, but this time he promised *me*."

It would be a mistake to ridicule this attitude of
mind as that of a vain and foolish old gentleman.
Mr. Chamberlain was sixty-nine at the time. But
he was not and is not either vain or foolish. He is a
tough old business man, of great vitality and fibre,
who has spent his life out in the world interviewing
men and assessing characters. He is a person of
immense experience.

It is true that his belief in Hitler's change of heart
must have been based on a belief in the power of a

glance from his own magnetic eye. For, at the three interviews, Mr. Chamberlain could only look at the Führer. Other means of communication were indirect. All conversation had to be conducted through an interpreter.

Just the same, Mr. Chamberlain, who was not in the habit of making errors in his assessment of human nature, was convinced that Hitler meant to play ball. He felt sure that the German Führer would never go to war against Britain now. Moreover that he would never go marching into the homes of any of his neighbours without consulting the British Prime Minister.

This act of faith achieved by a man whose judgment of his fellow creatures was respected even by his political opponents, had an immense effect on the whole community.

The Golden Age was born. For six months, after Munich, the great mass of the British politicians spent their time telling us that all was well, that Hitler was tamed, that the tiger had been transmogrified into a tabby by that old wizard of Number 10 Downing Street.

Citizens who pointed out that in October Hitler's Press had launched a savage campaign against Britain; that Hitler's thugs, about the same time, were forcing hundreds of elderly Jews to clean out public latrines, to dance in the streets clad in religious garments, or to expose their naked bodies in the cold wind; that such deeds indicated that the tabby still possessed tiger's claws, were denounced as Jitterbugs.

They were reviled and ridiculed. It was a really unpopular business to call Hitler a liar during the winter of 1938–1939.

People who did so were treated by their fellow men in much the same fashion as would be passengers on a pleasure cruise who went about the ship saying that, although the seas now were calm, they felt certain the captain had made a fatal error of navigation which would inevitably dash the liner on the rocks before another dawn.

Sir Archibald Southby, that gallant old Jack Tar with a face beaten by weather into the colour of rum, who represents Epsom in the Tory interest, caught the spirit of the day when he observed, "Is it true that the *bona fides* of the German Government is so poor? I do not believe it. I believe that to Herr Hitler peace for his people is an essential."

Mr. Herwald Ramsbotham clapped his monocle in his eye and contributed the comment, "We do not expect war, either now or in the near future."

The City caught the fever. At Lloyd's in December 1938 they were laying odds at 32 to 1 against Britain being involved in war before December 1939.

In November, Mr. Chamberlain hulloaed on the hounds who were chasing this trail by saying at the Guildhall, "Europe is settling down to a more peaceful state."

In his New Year's message to the people, Mr. Chamberlain mentioned the agreement with Italy, the piece of paper which Hitler had signed, the agreement with Eire and the American trade agreement and said, "A year marked by such underlying goodwill is one which leaves behind it no grounds for pessimism."

Mr. Edgar Granville, the Liberal National member for Eye, climbed on to a platform in his constituency and, rolling about like a sailor, as he always does when making a speech, roared, "Why all the jitters?"

A heckler in the crowd yelled back, "We're not frightened about Adolf, we're frightened about you, Edgar. Keep away from the edge of the platform or you'll roll off."

Over in America, Mr. Henry Ford remarked to a newspaper reporter, "I'll bet anybody even money there'll never be another war."

In South Africa, General Smuts said, "I think we are in for years of peace and quiet."

Mr. J. H. Thomas, after careful cogitation and after dinner too, stood up and gave forth, "I believe there will be no war."

Sir John Simon told the world, "There is a growing confidence in the preservation of peace." Even Mr. Eden, who hated the Munich agreement, was sufficiently infected by the prevailing atmosphere to thump on the table and exclaim, "War can be averted."

This Golden Age of confidence was produced in the minds of the politicians, as we have seen, by a belief in Hitler's word.

It was fostered in the minds of the public by a belief in the word of the British Government. Everyone supposed that British rearmament was approaching a thunderous crescendo.

On February 22, 1939, Mr. Chamberlain spoke. He said, "Our arms are so great that, without taking into account the Dominions' contribution

> *'Come the three corners of the world in arms*
> *And we shall shock them.'* "

Sir Samuel Hoare echoed his master's voice. He cursed the Jitterbugs, and said, "these timid panic-mongers were doing the greatest harm". He added,

"In the past we have been unprepared. I admit it. But I claim today that our preparations have already progressed to a formidable point."

On March 10, 1939, Sir Samuel once more exhorted the public to be of good cheer. "The long period of preparation (of armaments) has come to an end, and the results are now emerging with ever-increasing effect. I am convinced we could not be defeated in a short war by any knockout blow and that in a long war our almost inexhaustible resources will ensure the final victory."

Sir Samuel then proceeded to give his reasons why war, in any case, was not to be our lot or portion. He specifically named the approaching Golden Age and drew the blue print for it. We must have a Five Year Plan worked out by Five Men in Europe, "the three Dictators, and the Prime Ministers of Britain and France".

These men might make themselves "the eternal benefactors of the human race". Their plan would be based on peace, and its adoption would permit of efforts to create "a Golden Age with standards of living raised to heights we had never before been able to attempt".

.   .   .   .   .

Five days after this remarkable oration the whole earth shook and trembled as, without warning, Hitler's tanks smashed their way in thousands into Prague.

The British Government were pledged and bound to defend the new, truncated Czechoslovakia against aggression. Ever since Munich they had been assuring the public that they were ready, aye, ready now for the war which was never going to come.

It did not come then.

The British Government ran out on its pledge. In the light of the account which has been given of the state of armaments of the British Expeditionary Force stranded on the blood-soaked dunes of Dunkirk *more than a year later*, it may be that they had no choice.

Czechoslovakia vanished overnight. So did the Golden Age.

E M

CHAPTER XI

THE GRAND MISALLIANCE

OR THE COUNTRY OF WHICH HE KNEW NOTHING

THE CAST:

Neville Chamberlain, Sir John Simon, Sir Samuel Hoare

THE GOLDEN AGE was the shortest on record even in this era of rosy millenniums ended by Nazi surprises. Appeasement likewise was dead. But it still took some fifteen days to lie down.

Hitler had torn the Munich agreement to tatters by his march to Prague and while he was still parading through the streets of that unhappy capital the British Parliament met to hear Mr. Chamberlain's judgment. It was a most curious and contradictory display.

The Premier seemed confused. In the debate after Munich he had prophesied that Czechoslovakia would enjoy a greater security than she had ever known before and of course Sir John Simon and Sir Samuel Hoare had improved on their leader with their pictures of a new state as safe as Switzerland and guaranteed by a British pledge.

Now that the security of this state had been utterly disrupted, the Premier seemed to take a different view. "The attempt," he said, "to preserve a state containing Czechs, Slovaks as well as minorities and other nationalities, was liable to the same possibilities of change as was the constitution which was drafted when the state was originally framed under the Treaty of Versailles. And it has not survived. That may or may not have been inevitable, but I have so often heard charges of breach of faith bandied about which did not seem to me to be founded on sufficient premises, that I do not associate myself today with any charges of that character."

As the comment of a British Prime Minister on the extinction of a state which Britain had guaranteed that was hardly adequate. Members of the House shifted uneasily in their seats. They waited for something better, some expression of the British people's rising temper of indignation. They waited in vain.

Czechoslovakia unfortunately had "become disintegrated". It had come to pieces in Hitler's hands and Mr. Chamberlain as the charitable mistress of the House was in no mood to issue reprimands. "I am bound to say," he continued, "that I cannot believe anything of the kind which has now taken place was ever contemplated by any of the signatories to the Munich agreement at the time of its signature."

What had occurred was "bitterly regretted", but the Government had no intention of allowing these events to deflect them from their course. When the Premier resumed his seat, the House had the uneasy impression that appeasement was still alive and might still attempt to kick.

Sir John Simon in the concluding speech of the debate enforced that impression. He always strutted proudly into difficulties out of which his wiser companions were ready to sneak. It was his steadfast ambition to out-Chamberlain Chamberlain. The opposition had urged throughout the debate that these events in Prague must persuade the Government to abandon the policy of separate negotiation with the probable enemies of peace and to institute instead "the peace front" policy of alliance with the probable friends of peace.

Sir John Simon sought to kill any such plan. He set his bald pate and beady eye squarely against it. "It is really essential," he said, "that we should not enter into an extensive, general, undefined commitment with the result, to a large extent, that our foreign policy would depend, not on this country, this Parliament, and the Electors, but on a lot of foreign Governments."

That debate took place on Wednesday, March 15th. Two days later Mr. Chamberlain went to Birmingham to address his constituents. He reaffirmed Sir John's pronouncement: "I am not prepared," he said, "to engage this country by new unspecified commitments under conditions which cannot be foreseen." Yet his temper and certainly his tone were clearly changing. The protest against the seizure of Prague was more severe. "Is this the end of an old adventure, or is it the beginning of a new? Is this the last attack on a small state, or is it to be followed by others? Is this, in fact, a step in the direction of an attempt to dominate the world by force?"

The applause of his audience at these unaccustomed strong words seemed to answer his question. Amid thunderous clapping he concluded with a threat of the resistance which would be shown by a nation that valued peace, but that valued freedom even more.

Those words echoed round the land. They spoke the mind of the British people. A growing body of opinion believed that the first task of the Government now was to go out in search of allies who would stand with us against any further ravages of Nazi-ism. Where could those allies be found?

Hitler had written in *Mein Kampf* that the chief mistake of the rulers of Germany in 1914 was to have engaged in a war on two fronts. Should not, therefore, the first aim of those who sought to constrain Nazi Germany by the superior power of a peace alliance be to ensure that an alliance should be achieved embracing nations on both German fronts? It was the plain course. And the second simple principle must be that a strong ally was worth more than a weak ally. The strong should be sought first. That, too, was obvious wisdom.

The nation was hopeful. Had not the Russians, the strongest power to the east of Germany, proposed a conference at Bucharest of all powers interested in opposition to Nazi designs? The British Foreign Office had described that proposal as "premature". But surely there was still a good chance. Feeling was rising in the country. The Government was wavering. Surely something could be done.

It was in these circumstances that the British House of Commons assembled on March 31st, sixteen days after Hitler's entry into Prague, to hear the most amazing and momentous pronouncement of modern times. Mr. Chamberlain rose in his place, the same place where sixteen days earlier he had sworn that events in Prague would not be allowed to deflect the Government's policy from its previous course. He announced that "in the event of any action which clearly threatened Polish independence, and which the Polish Government accordingly considered it vital to resist with their national forces, His Majesty's Government would feel themselves bound at once to

GUILTY MEN

lend the Polish Government all the support in their power".

Poland was certainly threatened by Nazi power. It was also, like Czechoslovakia, a far-away country of which Mr. Chamberlain, it seemed, knew nothing. It was a country ruled by a degenerate crew of landowners and old soldiers, many of whom have since been convicted of treason to their state and the people they ruled. They had intrigued with the Nazis up to as late as March 1939. They had joined with the Nazis in the plunder of Czechoslovakia. Worst of all, for years they had been on bad terms with the Russians. They had steadfastly refused to enter the Franco-Soviet Mutual Assistance Pact. In the eyes of the Russians, who were in the best position to know, their army was considered weak and ineffective. It was to this nation, without consulting the Russians, that the British Government gave a guarantee. To this Government, in the words of Sir John Simon, "an extensive, general, undefined commitment" was given "with the result, to a large extent, that our foreign policy would depend, not on this country, this Parliament and the Electors", but on the views of a few irresponsible Polish leaders.

There is no record that Sir John Simon made a single protest against the new policy which he had so fiercely condemned a fortnight before. Not a word, not a cheep came from him. He cheered with the rest. Yet his first prophecy was correct. This bastard caricature of collective security produced to satisfy a public and a Commons which had hoped for the birth of a real collective security with powerful nations bedevilled our relations with Russia throughout subsequent months.

The Poles were partly able to dictate the terms on which an alliance between Moscow and London might be concluded. More and more clearly the Russians saw the spectre of German tanks crashing across the Polish plains, with the Polish armies crumbling before them, with the Allies in the West giving only that inconsiderable degree of aid which geography permitted—and with the Russian armies left to meet the full blast. The Russians said that, and Marshal Voroshilov, Chief of Staff, plainly saw it. Secretly, nefariously, the Soviet Government began to talk with the Germans.

This story can only be told briefly and some readers may dispute the argument. Rule it out if you wish. Whatever the truth of the Russian negotiations, with or without Russian aid, the inescapable facts were plain. Appeasement was pronounced dead. Britain was seeking Allies against Nazi aggression in a manner which previously her rulers had abjured. With or without Russia we were committed to War against Nazi-ism at any moment when the Polish Government believed their independence threatened.

Mr. Lloyd George asked if the General Staff had agreed to this acceptance of the guarantee of a frontier in the east of Europe which we could not easily reach and when at that time we had no Allies who could easily reach it. He got no answer. Mr. Chamberlain and his Cabinet were satisfied presumably that we could discharge the extraordinary obligation which we had undertaken. At very least he must have been satisfied that we had time enough to bring our defences into a satisfactory position.

Here then is the final fact. On March 31st, 1939, the people of this country were directly committed by their rulers to war against all the might of the German

Reich in easily foreseeable circumstances. Whatever the failure in equipping our defences hitherto, whatever our failure to take warning from successive events in the Rhineland, Abyssinia, Austria, Spain, Czechoslovakia, there could be no excuse now. The Government could only be justified in undertaking this great commitment if we pledged our all to the most terrific exertions to equip the nation for war in every department. They must be satisfied that the very best was done on land, in the air, at sea, in supply, agriculture and all other departments. That was the simple duty of our rulers to the people whose lives they had pledged.

On the day that he foreshadowed the pledge to Poland, Mr. Chamberlain indicated that this duty would be done. "In our country," he said, "we must review the position with that sense of responsibility which its gravity demands. Nothing must be excluded from that review which bears upon the national safety. Every aspect of our national life must be looked at again from that angle. The Government, as always, must bear the main responsibility, but I know individuals will wish to review their own position, too."

Mark, first, the date. *March, 1939*, sixteen months before the retreat to Dunkirk. (How many airplanes can be built in sixteen months? "Why didn't they send more?" asked the footsore soldiers.) Mark next those phrases: *Nothing must be excluded.* (Does that include tanks?) *Every aspect.* (Does that exclude fighters?)

Fifteen months after that pledge was given, seven months after Poland had been rolled off the map by Nazi tanks and bombers, Mr. Lloyd George, the man who had asked whether the General Staff approved the pledge, the man who pleaded for an agreement with

Russia first, rose in the House of Commons and asked this question:

> "*Is there anyone in this House who will say that he is satisfied with the speed and efficiency of the preparations in any respect for air, for Army, yea for the Navy?*"

He waited seconds for an answer. None came. The House was utterly silent. Among those who kept their seats were Mr. Chamberlain, Sir John Simon and Sir Samuel Hoare.

CHAPTER XII

CALIGULA'S HORSE

THE CAST:

The Horse	*Sir Thomas Inskip*
	(now Lord Caldecote)
Caligula	*Stanley Baldwin*

BRITAIN WAS NOW pledged to fight for Poland, a peasant nation at the far end of Europe.

The British public suspected that the Polish Government was corrupt and incompetent. They knew that while Beneš of Czechoslovakia was an irreconcilable opponent of Nazi methods Beck of Poland spent most of his spare time pottering around Berlin with leading figures of the Nazi movement.

They remembered that when the carcass of Czechoslovakia lay bleeding on the ground, the Poles had sprung in with Hitler's connivance and bitten off a great joint from the spoil.

That was about the total of knowledge the British public had of Poland. Just the same, having rejoiced at Chamberlain's refusal to aid the Czechs, the British people applauded loudly his decision to assist the Poles.

They were in fighting mood. Hitler's march had goaded them into a spirit of vengeance. Even Mr. Chamberlain, after that March episode, is said to have remarked to Sir Horace Wilson: "I can't believe it. I feel as if I had been cheated at cards."

It was plain that Hitler was about to turn on Poland and bully her. Danzig and the Polish Corridor; these were to be Hitler's next "last territorial demands in Europe".

In these circumstances, the strength of Britain's armaments became the most important consideration of every man of goodwill in these islands.

People looked anxiously back through the months and years. They pondered in their minds the value of Britain's rearmament programme. . . .

Mr. Churchill, for years, had been the dancing dervish of rearmament. He had foamed and challenged and ranted with impatience at the delay. He had been rebuked by Mr. Chamberlain. ("Among Mr. Churchill's very great qualities I cannot find that judgment is pre-eminent.") He had been sneered and jeered at by Mr. Baldwin.

Mr. Churchill had already taken the view that until some man was given the duty of co-ordinating the requirements of the three defence services, no real progress in rearmament could be made. The Premier of those days, Mr. Baldwin, had, in straight terms, rejected the suggestion.

But in the first week of March, 1936, public suspicion that the problem of rearmament was only being played with reached a point which aroused even that Premier. A big debate on rearmament was due to take place next week. Baldwin let it be known that a new Minister was to be given control of Britain's rearmament effort.

Everyone supposed Churchill would be the choice of Mr. Baldwin. This supposition quickened into a certainty in the public mind when, over the week-end of March 8, 1936, Hitler repudiated Locarno (which he had sworn to observe in spirit and letter) and sent his troops into the Rhineland.

Down to the House of Commons to debate rearmament came Members of all parties in a condition of high excitement. Sir Archibald Sinclair asked Mr. Baldwin if he would reveal the name of the new Defence Minister. Mr. Baldwin refused. He said he would not give the name until the debate was over. For he was asking the House of Commons to consider the merit of the new scheme for co-ordination of defence, not the Minister entrusted with the task of carrying it out.

For two days the debate continued. Members of all parties lined up behind Baldwin who told the House little about the rearmament but uttered hard and harsh words on the behaviour of the French. (The French were saying that we should go into the Rhineland and kick the Germans out again. We know now that Hitler's troops of entry had orders to withdraw into Germany at once if they met any opposition. The French did not carry out their plan because Baldwin and Britain told them they would do it at their peril and without any support from us.)

After the debate, M.P.s went home still convinced that Mr. Churchill was to be the new Minister of Defence. Instead, on Sunday, the 13th of March, Mr. Baldwin announced from No. 10 Downing Street that Sir Thomas Inskip was the man.

The reaction of a famous statesman when the news was brought to him was to observe "It is a clerical error". In the smoke-rooms of Westminster, he is said to have remarked, "there has been no similar appointment since the Roman Emperor Caligula made his horse a Consul".

When the appointment was posted up in the lobby of the House of Commons, Members of Parliament, House of Commons officials and journalists, burst into loud laughter. One aged lobby correspondent tumbled off his chair in a corner and fainted.

Lord Salisbury said in the House of Lords: "My confidence is shaken a little bit. I must confess I am surprised at the appointment."

Sir Austen Chamberlain also criticised the nomination, and said: "Mr. Churchill has great courage, infinite energy and great and wide experience in the matter of defence. Many in the House of Commons regret that Mr. Baldwin has not thought fit to call him to the office to which he has greater qualifications than any living politician."

The *Observer* remarked: "A more admirable man was never appointed to a more inappropriate office. Were the times more amusing it might be taken as the most diverting case on record of putting square pegs into round holes."

Sir Thomas Inskip himself appeared to entertain doubts as to his own capacity. Making his first speech in his new position he said: "I may say, with all sincerity, that it never occurred to me that I was likely to be asked to accept these responsibilities. Nor did it ever occur to me—I can say this in all seriousness—that I would ever be able to discharge these duties even if they were offered to me. . . . I do not claim to be a superman."

Sir Thomas was, in fact, a moderately successful barrister. Aided by family connections (he married a daughter of a seventh Earl), he went into politics. He had, by hard toil and easy fortune, worked his way up to the position of Attorney-General ("No one would call the Attorney-General a Moltke" observed the *Morning*

Post, when the new job was given to Sir Thomas), but he had never held a Cabinet position before.

Sir Thomas was, and is, a godly man, proud of the fact that he is a puritan. His enemies refer to him as "that bum-faced evangelical".

Sir Thomas has put it on record that he got down on his knees on that March evening, 1939, and prayed for divine help in the work of rearming Britain.

Next morning they gave him one room, one chair, and one secretary. He set to work.

CHAPTER XIII

CALIGULA'S RACE HORSE

THE CAST:

Sir Thomas Inskip

SIR THOMAS'S CRITICS continued to poke a little fun at him after his appointment. Mr. Churchill, for example, remarked that Sir Thomas was quite correct in claiming that the Army was being mechanised, "in the sense that its horses are being taken away from it".

Indeed, for a period Sir Thomas's doubts about his own capacity endured. "Sometimes I do not feel very well equipped for my office," he sadly said in May, 1936. But that is the last occasion on record when the Co-ordinating Minister expressed any feelings except satisfaction about his rearmament of Britain.

In 1937 he said: "I hope we shall never again as a nation make the mistake of allowing our defences to fall into a state of disrepair which I am afraid was the case up to two years ago."

By the beginning of 1938, Sir Thomas Inskip (nick-named 'Honest Tom' by his fellow barristers) was being criticised, in his capacity as Co-ordinating Minister, for not exerting himself more on behalf of the nation.

He therefore gave interviews to newspaper men. He gave out assurances that only those ignorant of the true position could feel any uneasiness about Britain's re-armament programme.

He announced these facts:

(1) *Air Force :* In many cases the programme was
far ahead of schedule. A minority of contractors had
fallen behind schedule in the building of air frames
though we had more engines than we could deal
with.

(2) *Raw Materials :* The community would be aston-
ished if they knew the huge reserves of raw materials
collected by the Government. As an example—we had
accumulated huge supplies of tungsten and wolfram,
both vital necessities for armaments.

(3) *Oil :* In every part of the Empire vast under-
ground storage reservoirs were already filled.

Also a comprehensive scheme had been made to turn
over all civil transport to gas-producing vehicles in
time of war, leaving the petrol for the army.

(4) *Navy :* The building programme was leaping
forward.

(5) *Army :* Factories to produce mechanised equipment for the army in immense quantities were almost
complete.

Sir Thomas Inskip gave the most solemn under-
takings that the tales that we were making bad progress
with rearmament were not true.

By the end of 1938, Sir Thomas appeared completely
contented with his own achievement. Here are his
utterances for that period:

Oct. 12th: "Mr. Churchill has spoken about Ethelred
the Unready. There is nothing unready about the
Air Force . . . our citizens do not want to be hood-
winked . . . I believe that we have at last got on the
road to friendly relations with Germany."

Oct. 26th: "Now we are at the middle of the third year
of rearmament there is in almost everything—I think
I may say everything—a stream which might fairly

be called a flood of these armaments and equipment which we need to complete our defences."

In December at Stoke-on-Trent, Sir Thomas was reported to say:

"Britain possesses the best anti-aircraft defences in the world."

Next day he sharply corrected this announcement, saying he had been misrepresented.

Finally let us leave Sir Thomas with the saying he poured through his pursed lips on August 3, 1939. "War today is not only not inevitable but is unlikely. The Government have good reason for saying that."

One of the reasons was said to be the state of preparedness which Sir Thomas had given us.

Was Sir Thomas a good Defence Minister? He held the job for three vital years.

CHAPTER XIV

THE MAN WITH THE SNOW SUIT

THE CAST:

Mr. Chamberlain, Earl Baldwin of Bewdley and Mr. Leslie Burgin

WHEN A CHILD swallows a button, you seize it by the legs, hold it head downwards, and shake it with violence. You bang its back. The child's face goes red, it screams and then chokes. But not until it is on the point of extinction will it surrender the button.

British Governments of the last few years have been much like a child with a button in its gullet. They have had to be shaken and banged by public opinion until they are on the point of destruction, before they will yield the smallest item.

The history of the creation of a Ministry of Supply illustrates this proposition. It needed four years of the most active and desperate activity on the part of critics of the administration, and the Government had to be slapped and kicked and cursed and brought to a point where its destruction seemed imminent, before it yielded to the clamour for a Ministry of Supply.

Mr. Baldwin, during the whole of his Premiership, stood like a policeman with uplifted arm forbidding any advance along the road which led to such a Ministry. Perhaps he took special delight in doing so because Mr. Churchill was the driver of the leading vehicle waiting to proceed in that direction. But although Mr. Churchill and his friends honked their horns, P.C. Baldwin stood fast, with a scowl of disapproval in their direction.

After Caligula's horse had been set up as Defence Minister, Mr. Churchill turned his attention to that gentleman. With the most appealing tone, he suggested that the horse would find it easier to struggle up the long hill of rearmament, if part of his burden was lifted from his back by the setting up of the Supply Ministry. Caligula's horse neighed an answer in the House of Commons on July the 8th, 1936. He said that in the view of the Government a Minister of Supply would not be "calculated to facilitate or increase the rate of the completion of the Government programme of rearmament".

The root of the Government's objection to the creating of a Supply Minister was a double one. Both, of course, could have been overcome had the Government cared to mobilise public opinion on the issue, and in any event should have been overcome with or without public opinion.

In November 1936, the Royal Commission which had been sitting for eighteen months, on the question of whether or not the arms industry should be nationalised, hatched out an egg in the shape of a report. This report recommended the setting up of a Ministry of Munitions, which would in effect have all the power of a Ministry of Supply.

In May 1937, the Cabinet turned down flatly this recommendation of the Commission which they themselves had set up.

For more than a year the struggle went on to induce the Government to give the country what every armament maker knew was necessary if we intended to race Germany's multiplication of arms.

In May 1938, the Government adopted a new line of defence. Lord Zetland, speaking for the administration in the House of Lords, said that we had, in effect, a Ministry of Supply already. This utterance of the noble lord was taken to be a reference to the efforts of Caligula's horse as Co-ordinating Minister.

After Munich, Earl Baldwin of Bewdley arose and made his maiden speech in the House of Lords. "I would mobilise industry tomorrow," said the Earl of Bewdley. In the House of Commons Mr. Churchill retorted with justice that Baldwin had the chance to mobilise industry during all those yesterdays when he held the premiership of Britain.

"He says he would mobilise tomorrow," declared Mr. Churchill. "I think it would have been much better if Earl Baldwin had said that two and a half years ago when everyone demanded a Ministry of Supply."

Mr. Chamberlain refused to set up a Ministry of Supply (November 1, 1938) on quite new grounds. He declared that such a Minister would have the effect of slowing down the progress of rearmament because he would dislocate the existing arrangement, which was working splendidly.

Five months later (April 20, 1939) the same Mr. Chamberlain came down to Parliament and announced that he had taken the decision to set up a Ministry of Supply, because he felt that such a Ministry would accelerate Britain's effort to rearm.

Then a sound like the escape of gas from a barrage balloon arose from the packed benches of Westminster and as it penetrated to the outer lobby took on the profounder note of a human moan.

It was the sound of M.P.s gasping when Mr. Chamberlain announced the name of the new Minister —Leslie Burgin. The announcement was greeted with as much astonishment as if Mr. Chamberlain had informed the House that he was about to despatch the Duke and Duchess of Windsor on a mission of friendship to Australia.

Did Burgin do a good job of work? For thirteen months he was responsible for producing equipment, uniforms, guns and tanks, destroyers and bombs and aircraft, to meet the requirements of our defence services.

Just after British troops sailed to Norway the Minister of Supply was photographed holding a white snow suit in his hand. He was reported to say that no British Expeditionary Force had ever left our shores so well equipped.

But the men of the Dunkirk beaches needed no snow suits. Their requirements were of a heavier nature.

CHAPTER XV

WHAT'S THERE BEHIND THE ARRAS?

See Hamlet

THE CAST:

Sir Horace Wilson

WHEN MR. CHAMBERLAIN flew to Germany to meet Hitler, he did not take with him the Foreign Office experts. He was content to be accompanied by the gentleman who was then known as Industrial Adviser to the Government. This figure is never seen without an umbrella (and it is still in dispute whether he gave the habit to Chamberlain or Chamberlain to him).

His name is Sir Horace Wilson. He deserves a prominent part in this narrative. For his was the policy, his the philosophy of life, his the ideology which dominated the mind of Mr. Chamberlain during the whole of his fateful Parliament.

Sir Horace Wilson established an ascendancy over Mr. Chamberlain which will take its place in history. Neither of the men were fully aware of the position. Yet things came to a point when no major decision of any kind was taken by the British Government before Sir Horace was consulted. If the plan did not win his approval it was often shelved.

Sir Horace Wilson for over two years was at any rate the second most powerful figure in the public life of this country. Yet he remains almost unknown to the general public. For Sir Horace is a Civil Servant. On that account he is, by tradition, exempt from the hurly-burly of political criticism and assault.

Indeed, on the few occasions when men in the know tried to point a finger at what they regarded as a pernicious influence in the public life of Britain, Mr. Chamberlain became enraged and called to the defence of his favourite and friend the tradition that Civil Servants cannot be attacked.

But the tradition is based on the belief that Civil Servants are only the instruments which carry out a policy formulated by the public men. Sir Horace Wilson, on the other hand, often saw the British Prime Minister converting himself into the instrument for carrying through a policy formulated by himself. On that account he should not be shrouded from the searchlight of public comment.

Sir Horace enjoyed immense power during the Premiership of Mr. Chamberlain. He was answerable to no one except the Prime Minister. He had a room next door to his patron and colleague at the Treasury. They went walking each day together.

It was fortunate for Britain that Sir Horace, with all his errors of judgment, is a man of integrity and with single purpose, the welfare of the state. If the man who wielded such huge influence in these years of destiny had been unpatriotic, the consequences would have been utterly irreparable.

Sir Horace's rise to power is a wonderful story. His father was a furniture dealer. His mother kept a boarding-house. Sir Horace was born in a Bournemouth back street. He went to the local board school. In course of time he got into the Civil Service, as a Second Division man. That is to say, he did not enter the Service in the top grade, which is expected to provide Civil Servants who plan the execution of policy. The second grade of the Civil Service is designed to provide the executive. It is an easy standard to achieve. The examination for the grade is open to those who have reached the advanced stages of a Secondary School education.

Sir Horace had his first big chance as a Civil Servant when the Labour Government came to power in 1929. Mr. J. H. Thomas formed a high opinion of his abilities. He pulled him into the band-waggon when Mr. Mac-Donald's Government, improving on Lloyd George's slogan, said, "We *will* conquer unemployment!"

But when it became clear that neither Mr. Thomas nor Sir Horace could, in fact, conquer unemployment, Sir Horace was out of a job himself. He was shoved on one side and given the title "Economic Adviser to the Government", which meant very little at that time.

When the Ottawa Conference took place in 1932, the British Members needed a Civil Servant to travel with them. As Sir Horace was at large, they took him. It was during this Conference that he established his grip over Mr. Chamberlain. He saw clearly, with the clarity that often accompanies narrow vision. By the time the con-ference was at an end, Mr. Chamberlain (at that time Chancellor of the Exchequer) was placing complete faith in the judgment of Sir Horace.

Since then (until Mr. Churchill became Premier) Sir Horace has reigned. He had a good deal to do with the arrangement which ended in the Abdication of the Duke of Windsor. As we have seen, he was in the heart of the Munich negotiations.

His eyes are pale blue, he seldom smiles, never jokes, and has never been heard to reply to a question with a plain "Yes" or "No". He married a farmer's daughter three years older than himself. They have three children.

On Sunday, he is a sidesman at St. Mary's Church, Chorley, Sussex, acting turn and turn about with a local shop assistant. At one time he was said to be greatly interested in the Oxford Group movement. Some people believe that he has sympathy with the doctrines of Dr. Buchman. But that has never been established. When a reporter tried to question Sir Horace on the issue, he did not answer and behaved as though he had not heard the question.

Sir Horace has never been distracted from his opportunities by political expediences or considerations of personal advancement. He is only concerned with giving advice which he believes will benefit the country.

Since Mr. Chamberlain stepped down from the throne of Premiership, Sir Horace's influence in the affairs of the nation is necessarily curtailed. Sir Horace holds by no means the same position with the new Premier as he did with the old.

Just the same, he remains head of the Civil Service. He has perpetuated his position in that service to some extent. For during the last few years no Civil Servant stood much chance of being appointed to a key position in any department unless his political outlook coincided with that of Sir Horace.

What is that outlook? Sir Horace's whole temperament is that of an "appeaser". War, to him, is a silly business—so silly, that no sensible being, even a German dictator, would really undertake it, however much he might threaten to do so.

As a result of Sir Horace's leadership, the number of Civil Servants in Britain has been increased. The dead hand of bureaucracy grips us by the throat. It stifles and strangles with red tape all those who desire to take determined and drastic action.

The story is told of a Senior Civil Servant who wished to see a Junior Clerk, named Perkins, with a view to promoting him. He was conducted along a passage when through an open door he heard a voice saying: "What, you want another new nib? You only had one two days ago."

"Who is it?" asked the Senior Civil Servant. "Perkins, sir," was the answer. "Promote him," said the Senior, and turned back. . . . He had heard enough.

This story is in the best Wilson tradition.

CHAPTER XVI

DAVID

THE CAST:

Rt. Hon. Capt. Margesson, M.P., P.C., Govt. Chief Whip

How DID IT happen that, in all the years which were wasted, no serious parliamentary revolt took place against the administration?

There were men in Parliament—not many, but some —who realised we were drifting into catastrophe. There were scores of journalists and business men in the know who were convinced that the dead bureaucratic hand of the Civil Service, coupled with the complacent willingness of some of our Ministers to relax their exertions so long as they could keep the public quiet by pouring the soft and soothing oil of optimism over their heads, was putting us in peril.

Yet Parliament was quiescent. It remained acquiescent. During the whole period in which rearmament was alleged to be taking place, there was no serious revolt among the massed legion of the Tory back-benchers.

This remarkable situation was due to the efforts of one man, Captain David Margesson. He was, and is, Government Chief Whip.

Now, in the party system, a Whip can never take an objective view of events. His duty is simply to maintain his own party, right or wrong. He may sleep soundly in his bed if London is bombed, but will not do so if the Party has had "a bad day".

Fortunately for Captain Margesson, his duty and his inclination follow the same course.

He believes sincerely that the British aristocratic classes who form the head of the Tory party are more astute, more able, more gifted, more inspired than any other people in any country in the world. Perhaps he is right. Certainly he holds that belief with complete honesty and conviction.

Captain Margesson has performed his duties as Chief Whip to the Tories in a manner so absolute and so competent that it will take its place in history. Lloyd George, with fifty years of Parliament behind him, paid the Captain the deserved tribute of naming him the most efficient Chief Whip in his experience.

The Captain is a suave and handsome person, and at fifty he retains a youthful and graceful figure. Indeed the Captain exactly resembles a thoroughly efficient Sixth Form prefect who enjoys and earns the esteem of the Headmaster in managing the rest of the school. The Captain applies to the House of Commons Old School Tie Brigade the methods of a public school. If one of the "boys" has erred, or strayed into the wrong lobby, the rest of them will quickly be notified that the fellow is a bit of an outsider. And the friends of outsiders, in the public school code, are of course to be regarded as outsiders themselves.

If the cad still won't play the game, well he must be put in Coventry. The other chaps shun and spurn him, and shut up talking when he enters the room.

It is a remarkable reflection on the frailty of humanity that even a grown man can rarely "take it". In any event the "outsider" must reconcile himself to

the certainty that in offending the head prefect he has
put himself "outside" all prospect of becoming a prefect himself and of enjoying the favours which that
rank confers.

*   *   *   *   *

The Tory constituencies are controlled by the
Central Office at Palace Chambers. No official
Tory can employ in his constituency an agent who
does not possess a Central Office Certificate. This
certificate can be rescinded at will by Central Office.
So the effect is that, if an agent refuses to carry out the
instructions given him by Central Office, his certificate
can be withdrawn and he will thus be deprived of a
livelihood.

In fact, a Tory agent, though his member pays him
his salary, is the servant of Central Office at Palace
Chambers.

Now an agent usually has far more influence inside a
division than the Member. The agent is there all the
time. He lives among the people. He knows them all.
They will do things for him which they would not do
for the Member.

If Central Office desire to bring a rebel M.P. to
order they have the means. The M.P.'s own agent
is instructed to "test the strength of the party feeling"
against that rebel's act of indiscipline. If the result is
unfavourable—and it usually is—then it is the agent's
plain duty to inform the Member. And being naturally
on friendly terms with him the agent will add the
kindly advice, "But, sir, it would make it much easier
for me down here if you wouldn't oppose the Government *quite* so openly."

It will be seen from this account that Sir Kingsley Wood in his capacity of head of the Tory party machine could easily have crushed any Parliamentary movement against him in his capacity as Air Minister.

No doubt he would not have done so. In any case, it was never put to the test. There was never a serious revolt against him.

But Captain Margesson has developed into something more than a super-efficient head prefect. His power is more extensive than that of any of his predecessors at the Tory Whip's office.

Captain Margesson puts a list of Government speakers on the Speaker's chair at the beginning of every debate. So this man can help you to "catch the Speaker's eye".

He can advance men who fit in with him. In every Ministerial shuffle of the last five years, the Tory Chief Whip has been to the fore. Many of the men who have failed, as well as some who have succeeded, in the years which are gone, were set up on high by the insistency of Captain Margesson.

Finally, no Government Bill is presented to Parliament without consultation with the Chief Whip. He is asked how the House will take it. By his assurance Captain Margesson is able to mould policy.

He is, in fact, one of the most responsible individuals in British public life to-day, and has been so for a decade.

Only once has he lost his grip of the Tory backbenchers. That was when Mr. Chamberlain was thrown out of the Premiership by a hostile vote. Captain Margesson informed the then Premier that this vote was not going to be hostile.

But Captain Margesson made amends to Mr.

Chamberlain. He took a big part in the constitution of Mr. Churchill's new Government.

Mr. Chamberlain is still there. (Sir Kingsley Wood is Chancellor of the Exchequer, and retains control of the Tory party machine.)

And Captain Margesson is joint Chief Whip.

CHAPTER XVII

THEY HAD BEEN WARNED

THE CAST:

The British Cabinet

The Polish Cavalry

NAZI GERMANY CROSSED the frontier of Poland and the world went to war in September 1939. How many warnings had previously been issued to the rulers of Britain?

Hitler himself had written it in *Mein Kampf*; the million speeches delivered by the Nazi leaders on the hustings of Germany; the denunciation of Versailles; the institution of Conscription in Germany; the murder of Dollfuss; the murder of Barthou; the Rhineland; Spain; Austria; Czechoslovakia; Munich; Prague— these and countless more. How many further proofs were needed? Hitler gave the last supreme warning in the devastation of Poland.

The army of this people was supposed to inherit the traditions of Pilsudski. It had been praised by the military visitors from Paris and London. It went down inside a month before the bludgeoning assault of German tanks and German bombers. It was utterly obliterated. Its generals were sent racing for the Rumanian frontier. Its Commander-in-Chief, Marshal Smigly-Rydz (the name means "Lightning") was first across the line. Surely none after this could retain doubts or illusions.

A new method of war had been devised. A terrific accumulation of metal had succeeded in executing the new method. Poland was wiped clean off the map. Against this power which had done the deed Britain was committed to war to the end. All our honour and all our resources were pledged. Whatever the failings in the past, surely now the British people would be called upon to give their last ounce of energy.

All the facts of Germany's prodigious capacity for war were known. Mr. Churchill had reiterated them to the House of Commons over the previous years. No room was left for doubt. We knew the German aptitude for organisation. We knew the fury with which Hitler had shackled these aptitudes for his own purposes.

Eighty million people had been whipped until they devoted all their services to the business of preparation for war. For seven years the German people lived on iron rations and in barrack discipline. The manhood, the youth, the women laboured, drilled and lived to one end—war against the world. In the six years before September 1939, Germany had spent £6,000,000,000 on war preparations alone. Thus a terrific wealth for war was accumulated within the German Reich before that fateful September.

Poland gave the final evidence. The Nazi war machine was devastating, overwhelming. The mass of armoured columns ploughed through the herd of horses, the renowned Cavalry of Poland, which constituted the chief military arm of the semi-feudal state. The power of weapons in the air was proved beyond all quibble. Millions of Polish slaves were tied to the Nazi chariot. No one could doubt now that Nazi Germany was a formidable opponent. The total resources of Britain and France would be required to overturn it. So much was

GM

proved. It had all happened in the space of one month. The Polish Army was actually destroyed in eighteen days, the rest was a story of indomitable, abandoned garrisons.

No excuse for inaction remained now. Henceforth the rulers of Britain, if they knew their job, would summon all the resources of their empire to meet the assault. This was elementary responsibility. How did they discharge it?

So many times in these previous years they had promised that all was well. So many times they had promised that the power of our arms was growing in overwhelming proportions. The test must soon come. If there were any deficiencies they had their last chance— a chance so much longer than any could have calculated.

How did they employ this precious interval?

CHAPTER XVIII

PORTFOLIO WITHOUT A MINISTER

THE CAST:

Half Lord Stamp (the other half according to Lord Stamp's own profession was at the service of the railways)

WAR PREPARATION IS fundamentally a matter of economics. The Nazis had realised that. They had been spending prodigiously. In the year before the war they spent £1,650,000,000 on armaments alone.

Our rulers turned themselves to the task in a more leisurely manner. A clamour arose from Parliament and outside that Mr. Chamberlain should institute a small War Cabinet on the model of that which under Mr. Lloyd George had won the Great War of 1914–18.

Mr. Chamberlain sternly opposed the plan. He preferred to continue with the peace-time methods. Yet he was not unmindful of the necessity of satisfying the critics. Their chief grievance was directed against the failure to appoint a supreme economic minister capable of co-ordinating the various aspects of the nation's economic life in war time. Mr. Chamberlain then threw a sop in the form of Lord Stamp. He was to become the Government's Adviser on Economic Co-ordination. It was unfortunate that Lord Stamp could not give his whole mind to the business. He was also a director of the London, Midland and Scottish Railway. "I am giving a lot of time to the railway," said Lord Stamp some weeks after his appointment.

It was unfortunate, for the rest of the economic organisation of the nation for war was in the hands of Sir John Simon. He spoke on these matters in the counsels of the Cabinet. He represented the views of the Treasury. And he was successful in war as in peace in carrying through the Treasury policy of ensuring that expenditure should be rigorously limited.

Lord Stamp, despite his grandiose title of Economic Co-ordinator, discovered that his flimsy powers and his preoccupation on the railways prevented him from enforcing that total mobilisation for war which Herr Goering, Dr. Schacht, Dr. Funk and others had been introducing into Germany through the previous seven years.

What was the result of this half-baked, unco-ordin-ated scheme of economic mobilisation? It was revealed in Sir John Simon's budget of April 1940. In the first seven months of the war Britain spent at the rate of "four and a half millions a day". During the next six months it was proposed that the figure should be raised to five and a half millions a day and during the six months after that at the rate of five and three-quarter millions a day.

The momentum was not impressive and comparison with expenditure in Germany and France—frequently made in the House of Commons—revealed its in-adequacy. Germany was spending £3,200,000,000 a year. Britain was spending no more than £2,000,000,000. France and Germany each claimed three fifths of their national income for their war budgets; Britain claimed only two fifths.

Opposition M.P.s were aghast at this record. Mr. Amery in particular clamoured for a more urgent appreciation of the nation's need. Many pointed the remedy. They demanded a small War Cabinet in which one Economic Minister would sit charged with the task of directing the whole nation's economic effort. But Mr. Chamberlain was adamant. He would not change the system.

Thus through the first nine months of the greatest war in history Britain consistently spent less than her enemy by more than £1,000,000,000. It was hardly surprising that less money meant less arms. The soldiers who went to battle in Belgium with insufficient weapons to protect their bare bodies may find one explanation in the budget which Sir John Simon introduced in such complacent tones in the month of April 1940.

What was the cause of this strange delinquency? One was that Lord Stamp was only asked to give half his time to the job. Another was that Sir John Simon was determined to uphold the most rigid traditions of the Treasury. Another was, as Mr. Duff Cooper suggested in the House of Commons, that "Lord Hankey wouldn't like it". Another was that even after all the warnings, the devastation in Poland, the knowledge of the huge exertions which the Germans had made, after all these things our rulers were still unaware of the meaning of total war.

Whatever the true cause, the matter is academic. The soldiers of Britain had insufficient tanks and airplanes to protect them for the simple reason that insufficient money had been spent to buy them. It was not really Lord Stamp's fault. He was only half guilty. The nation's railways must be carried on.

CHAPTER XIX

MR. BROWN, NOT YET UNEMPLOYED

THE CAST:

Mr. Ernest Brown

ALL GERMANY WAS at work. All her millions of people had been at work for years. It was done by lash and boot, but none the less it was done. There was no unemployment. There was a shortage.

Between 1934 and 1938 the number of workers employed in Germany rose from just under 16,000,000 to 21,500,000—an increase of 5,500,000. The majority went into the armament industry. An even fiercer knout was applied to the new enslaved populations which Germany had conquered. Between March 1938 and May 1938 the numbers employed in Austria rose by 540,000. In the same period the numbers employed in Sudetenland rose by 180,000. Added to these were the newly conquered serfs of Poland. Not only all Germany, but all the new Nazi empire was at work. Night and day producing munitions of war.

The man in charge of the employment of the British people was Mr. Ernest Brown. He had different ideas. His chief complaint was against the weather. It caused the most distressing additions to his total of unemployed persons. Wet weather meant that the builders were out of work. Fine weather meant that the day's work could not properly be compared with what had preceded and what was to follow. For every season Mr. Ernest Brown had his seasonable excuses.

They were not always satisfactory. In December 1939, three months after the war had started, he had to admit that the unemployment total still remained at the 1,400,000 figure. It had increased by 172,000 since the war began. These figures included men who might have been considered essential to the nation's war production. At a time when the maximum agricultural population was considered essential, they included 28,000 agricultural workers. Mechanics were urgently needed; there were still 21,000 General Engineers and 20,000 men skilled in metal manufacture unemployed.

Germany was assessing her war needs in different terms. By April 1940, she had trained, since the beginning of the war, 500,000 men for semi-skilled and skilled work. Nearly 2,000,000 women had been taken into industry. The shortage of labour, even in this empire which had brought so many serfs under its control, was becoming acute. What had Mr. Brown to set against such a terrific outburst of energy?

The answer was given in May. In that month for the first time in years the British unemployment total fell below the million mark. The total now was 360,000 lower than in August 1939. Since many more than 360,000 had been called up into the British Army the reduction was not altogether remarkable.

There were still nearly a million unemployed persons in Britain in May 1940—the month of Hitler's invasion of Belgium. They might have been blind and crippled for all the contribution they were allowed to make to the national war effort. They were not idlers. In six years at the Ministry of Labour, through months of war, Mr. Brown was unable to find any use for their labours.

Not only did these citizens, disfranchised in the most heartbreaking way, contribute nothing to the nation. They were compelled to continue as a burden on it.

They wanted only to make weapons for the soldiers of Britain. Mr. Brown and his Government could not make use of their services. He was still lamenting the weather when he was removed from his office—to another post.

CHAPTER XX

HOW TO LOOK A FOOL

THE CAST:

Mr. W. S. Morrison and
Sir Reginald Dorman-Smith

FOOD WINS—AND loses—wars.

Blockade helped powerfully to defeat the Germans in the last war. Through anxious hours during 1917 we ourselves felt the potency of the weapon. Little more than a fortnight stood between us and disaster. In all the years that followed, therefore, the men who had seen the peril at the closest quarters warned and exhorted the nation.

The rot continued. Every year more acres went out of production and more workers left the land. We had four million more mouths to feed than in 1914. Yet compared with that year by 1938 our arable acreage was down by more than two million acres and the number of agricultural workers had fallen by 250,000. Lloyd George's voice rose ever louder in protest.

Others took a much less urgent view of the matter. Mr. W. S. Morrison warned the country against "a false fatalism". "I believe it is wrong for people to talk about war as if it were an inevitable calamity," he said. "What fools we should all look," he added, "if we interfered with the industry by building up an artificial system against a war that never happened." Mr. W. S.

Morrison was Minister of Agriculture. Lloyd George was a "disgruntled critic".

That speech was delivered in January 1938. Another year passed during which the decline continued. At last it was decided that Mr. Morrison should follow the example of his agricultural workers. He was removed to another employment. Sir Reginald Dorman-Smith, a gentleman farmer (but more a gentleman than a farmer), was to take his place. Great store was set on his appointment. Had he not sworn a few days before his elevation that agricultural production could be increased by £100,000,000 a year and a million men could be brought back to the land?

Sir Reginald faced his responsibilities with confidence. He had a plan for putting two million acres under the plough. He asked us to "dig for victory". He was optimistic about the feeding stuff situation. "There is no scarcity of feeding stuffs for livestock," he said on September 4, 1939, thereby successfully discouraging the winter sowing of cattle feed. "Future prospects of barley and maize for pigs and poultry are decidedly better than they have been," he added in January 1940, thus discouraging early spring sowing. So the optimistic story continued. Some disturbance was caused by the incorrigible Lloyd George. But had he not always been a "disgruntled critic"?

One Sunday in June 1940, a new voice spoke to the British farmers. In the months since September workers had continued to leave the land at the rate of some 8,000 a month. A grudging admission had been extorted from Mr. Morrison that: "There were no surplus feeding stuffs at the outbreak of war." These deficiencies had not worried the previous occupants of the office. But now a new Minister of Agriculture in a new Government announced a new policy. Something was to be done, which even Lloyd George would not fail to applaud. But first the unhappy legatee of Mr. Morrison and Sir Reginald Dorman-Smith had to deal with his bequest. The shortage of feeding stuffs would make it necessary to slaughter nearly a third of our pigs and poultry.

After nine months of combat there could no longer be any doubt that the war in preparation for which Mr. Morrison had refused "to interfere with the agricultural industry" had actually happened.

CHAPTER XXI

A FRIEND OF MR. CHAMBERLAIN

THE CAST:

Lord Stanhope

On November 8, 1939, Mr. Churchill as First Lord of the Admiralty rose in his place in the House of Commons to describe the circumstances of one of the early disasters of the war. A Nazi submarine had sailed into Scapa Flow and sunk the *Royal Oak*. Many brave sailors had lost their lives.

It was known long before the war started that the Fleet would be anchored at Scapa Flow. It was known that the enemy would send submarines in an attempt to penetrate its defences; in the last Great War five unsuccessful sallies had been made. The Navy had been mobilised in September 1938. From that day forward Scapa Flow should surely have been made impregnable. Yet Mr. Churchill told the House of Commons that one essential blockship only arrived a day after the sinking; that is, six weeks after the outbreak of war. Partly also the disaster was due to the fact that the patrolling craft were below strength in this chief of our naval anchorages.

The loss of brave sailors was not the only misfortune which we suffered owing to these delinquencies. Mr. Churchill explained some months later that the Fleet had been robbed of the use of Scapa Flow over a long period. Our ships had had "to undergo a great deal of unnecessary steaming in dangerous waters ". In fact our ships had been at sea more continually than was ever dreamed of in any previous war since the introduction of steam.

Who, then, was responsible? It was not Mr. Churchill. Sir Roger Keyes spoke in the debate. He told us that "in his opinion—and he was sure it was the opinion of the whole service—if Mr. Churchill had been in office before the war there would have been no question of any unreadiness in the Forces ".

Who was the man? The First Lord of the Admiralty on the outbreak of war was Lord Stanhope, seventh Earl, an old Etonian, a former Guardsman. The nation knew nothing of him except for a few silly speeches which he had delivered at various intervals and which it would be tedious to adumbrate.

Lord Stanhope was not removed from office when the scandal of Scapa Flow became known. He continued to draw £5,000 from the state as Lord President of the Council. Mr. Chamberlain still looked after his friends even if Lord Stanhope had failed to look after the sailors.

CHAPTER XXII

AN EPITAPH

CAST:

*Lord Baldwin, Mr. Chamberlain, Sir Kingsley Wood,
and Sir Samuel Hoare*

HERE IS AN epitaph which should be placed on the grave of every British airman killed in this war, every British civilian killed by Nazi bombers, every little child in this kingdom who may be robbed of life and happiness by high explosive or splintering metal rained down on this island by Marshal Goering's air force.

"His Majesty's Government are determined in no conditions to accept any position of inferiority with regard to what air force may be raised in Germany in the future."

These words we have met before in this story. They were spoken in the House of Commons. The date was November 28th, 1934. The speaker was Stanley Baldwin.

Five years later Britain and Germany went to war. In that September of 1939 Germany, according to a statement made by Mr. Chamberlain himself (May 7, 1940) was "far superior to us in arms and equipment". Her chief superiority, as no one will dispute, resided in the size of her air force. The essential military importance of that superiority was quickly revealed in Poland.

The delay in the previous five years was criminal enough. Surely now no more would be tolerated. There were rumours of continued inefficiency. The House of

Commons waited anxiously for an explanation. On March 7, Sir Kingsley Wood addressed the House.

It was naturally impossible to give figures. The M.P.s had either to believe or disbelieve the statements of the Minister according to their preference.

Sir Kingsley, however, was quite satisfied with the progress made. He said that the fighting strength of the R.A.F. had been increased 100 per cent during the previous twelve months. He added "with some confidence that even on a numerical basis the output of aircraft accruing to us and to France is to-day in excess of that of Germany."

These were high claims, but they were believed and applauded by the Conservative majority since these were days when Captain Margesson still ruled.

Others refused to believe Sir Kingsley's claims.

Among them were numerous M.P.s who asked for a precise meaning of the word "accruing".

Among them, too, was the *Times* newspaper (usually no hostile critic). "The figures given in these statements," wrote the *Times* on the day after the debate, "do not necessarily mean that the total production (which had reached a high level last September,) has yet increased at all," (that is, since the outbreak of war).

The *Times* had voiced the discontent of numerous sections of the public. The protest grew. At last Mr. Chamberlain bowed before it. Sir Kingsley was to be given a rest in another Cabinet post. A new Minister of Air was to be appointed. The name was announced. Who was the new titan, now to be charged with the greatest task of all?

Sir Samuel Hoare. The same Sir Samuel Hoare who had sat at Mr. Baldwin's elbow on that November day

in 1934 when he pledged the honour of all His Majesty's
Ministers to ensure that our power in the air should
never be allowed to become inferior to that of Germany.
The same Sir Samuel Hoare who sat on the Government bench through most of the intervening five years.
The same Sir Samuel Hoare who had twice previously
been Air Minister.

When the news of the appointment became known,
an aged opponent of the administration rose from his
seat, "This is where I came in," he said.

CHAPTER XXIII

MISSING THE BUS

THE CAST:

Mr. Chamberlain

IT WILL BE seen from the account of events here set out that the British Government did not exert itself to any great extent in the arming of our country, even after we had clashed into war with the most tremendous military power of all times.

The pressure on the Government not to do so came from Sir John Simon at the Treasury. His views were reinforced by the Banks, representing Big Business. The case for lethargy presented by these people was as follows:

"Do not disorganise industry by turning the whole country into an arms factory. Let us continue to manufacture pins and bicycles and films and vacuum cleaners so that we can make profits, contribute to taxation and pay for the war."

Tens of thousands of people in Britain became angry and indignant at this state of affairs. Young men, who wanted to fight, could not get called up. There were no guns for them. Young women who wanted to work at munition making could not do so. There were no new munition factories to absorb them.

Meanwhile, millions of tons of raw materials which could have been converted into instruments of war were manufactured into perambulators.

HM

In order to quieten the apprehensions of the citizens,
Ministers and generals began to make a series of
speeches calculated to encourage the public in the
belief that the war was already won.

On April 3, 1940, Mr. Chamberlain, still Prime
Minister, declared that he was ten times as confident of
victory as he was when the war began.

"*Whether it was that Hitler thought he might get away
with what he had got without fighting for it, or whether it
was that, after all, his preparations were not sufficiently complete, one thing is certain—HE MISSED THE BUS*"
said Mr. Chamberlain.

The Prime Minister added, "When war broke out
German preparations were far ahead of our own. It was
natural then to expect that the enemy would take ad-
vantage of his initial superiority, to make an endeavour
to overwhelm us and France before we had time to
make good our deficiencies. Is it not a very extraordinary thing that no such attempt was made? *Those seven
months that we have had have enabled us to make good and
remove our weaknesses ; to consolidate and tune up every arm,
offensive and defensive, and so enormously to add to our fighting
strength that we can face the future with a calm and steady
mind, whatever it brings.*"

On April 4, General Ironside joined the chorus.
General Ironside was at that time Chief of the Imperial
General Staff.

"Frankly we could welcome an attack," ejaculated
that old warrior. "We are sure of ourselves. We have
no fears. Our Army has at last turned the corner. I
was sure of this for the first time a fortnight ago. We
started with very little. The Germans gave us these
months to build a real fighting force. If they had
launched a full attack at the very start when we were

unprepared, they might possibly have got us. It's too late now. We are ready for anything they may start. As a matter of fact we'd welcome a go at them."

Within a week, the Germans overran Norway. So little did Mr. Chamberlain know of this invasion that he hinted to the expectant House of Commons that they must take with a grain of salt the tales that the Germans were in Narvik. Mr. Chamberlain himself took the view that the place in German hands might well be Larvik (a port 1,000 miles south down the coast of Norway).

"I have no doubt," added the ex-Prime Minister of Britain, "that this further rash and cruel act of aggression will redound to Germany's disadvantage and contribute to her ultimate defeat."

Two months later the last British troops were hurried home from Norway, and bombed as they departed by the Germans, who now possess the whole Norwegian coastline, with airfields for their planes and deep water harbours for their ships, so providing themselves with a first-rate opportunity to slip in and out through Britain's blockade, or to launch attacks on the Scottish coast.

Mr. Chamberlain added to his pep talks with this sentence spoken on April 15, 1940, to the National Free Church Council:

"Only a short while ago I declared that I felt ten times as confident as at the beginning of the war of ultimate victory. I repeat that confidence now."

.   .   .   .   .

On the morning of May 10, with a roar which drowned the futile boasts and foolish brags of Britain's Prime Minister and Chief of General Staff, the Nazi hordes streamed over the frontiers of Holland, Belgium and Luxemburg, with tanks, planes, guns and motorised infantry in endless columns.

Within three weeks the tragedy of the Dunkirk Beaches was enacted before the staring eyes of a trembling world.

CHAPTER XXIV

BLITZKRIEG

THE CAST:

The Supreme Commander-in-Chief of the German Armed Forces, A. Hitler

WHEN HITLER WAS threatening Czechoslovakia in September, 1938, Dr. Edouard Beneš, President of the country, apprised the British Government of the following information: Germany has five armoured divisions and Czechoslovakia has four. No notice was taken of this information.

I here raise in precise form the question I have asked in general terms in an earlier chapter: Was this statement put before the Staffs of the French and British armies? If it was, who rejected it? If it was not, why was it not?

On May 10, 1940, Hitler struck in the West with *blitzkrieg* fury. Head and front of the German onslaught were nine armoured divisions co-operating with innumerable airplane squadrons that consigned to the dustbin the assurances of Messrs. Baldwin, Chamberlain, Hoare and Kingsley Wood that we were either getting or had got "air parity".

The *blitzkrieg*. It means lightning-war. This was that *blitzkrieg* which Mr. Beverley Baxter, M.P., in his role of Government soothsayer, had assured his Sunday-dinner public in April, "threatened to become a comic epitaph".

"It is extremely unlikely that Germany will attack France" wrote Mr. Baxter three Sundays before the greatest war in the West. This Mr. Baxter is at present officially haranguing the British factory workers on the need for output to hold up the *blitzkrieg* which has laid mighty France, mangled and bleeding, by the roadside.

Generalissimo Hitler's onslaught was delivered in six waves against Holland and Belgium. The main strategy which directed the invasions was that which had so brilliantly served "Politicissimo" Hitler. Divide and Conquer. Divide and conquer Liberals, Socialists, Communists, Catholics, Conservatives. Divide and conquer Austrians, Czechs, England and France. The German armies thrust between the Dutch and the Belgians. The rest of the operation was to envelop the weaker army and compel its annihilation or surrender.

The military instrument Hitler employed was a completely merged and perfectly synchronised use of (a) motorised advance guard, (b) airplanes-cum-tanks, (c) motorised infantry-cum-artillery, (d) Fifth column treachery.

These tactics have been described as "revolutionary". This word conceals the surprise and the dismay with which our rulers faced them. In sober fact these tactics were derived and developed from the last war which Britain carried to a victorious conclusion in 1918.

In 1940 the newspapers suddenly became filled with discussion and explanation of the operation called "infiltration". Hitler's armoured divisions had thrown themselves suddenly and violently against the Allied positions and either by crossing yielded bridgeheads along the Albert Canal (Belgian) and the Meuse River

(French) or by expeditious and efficient pontooning had passed the river barriers and were "fanning-out" behind the Allied lines.

The tanks charged on—to Arras, Amiens, Abbeville, eventually to Boulogne and Calais. In none of these places did they encounter serious initial resistance—though later a hastily gathered garrison of battalions from the Rifle Brigade, 60th Rifles, Queen Victoria Rifles and the Tank Corps, in all 4,000 men, were flung into the citadel of Calais to cover the Dunkirk evacuation. They held it four days, and as far as we know thirty wounded men fell into the enemy hands alive.

At Arras German motor-cyclist troops swept into the town with Tommy guns on their handle-bars and seized the key points in a few hours. There were no line-of-communication troops to oppose them, and the railway station was eventually regained for a day or two by Sappers and Royal Army Service Corps armed with rifle and bayonet. At Abbeville, fifty miles behind "the front", the stationmaster was chatting to a British officer on leave when the German motor-cyclists rode up and relieved him of his duties.

But really there was nothing "revolutionary" in all this. In 1915 the intelligent French Infantry captain, André Laffargue, had already discerned the principle of "infiltration" which simply means that when your attack is held up by a few strong points you pass around and beyond them, like a tide washing in against rocks. It was the Germans who first employed this (then really revolutionary) idea to the full. In March, 1918, their infantry waves poured through the Allied defences. *All that Hitler has done is to speed up the tides.*

Hitler has put the first wave of infantrymen on motor-cycles. He has given them, in the shape of tanks, a mechanised ram to smash in the enemy front. Instead of the old barrage of shells from more or less stationary field batteries, Hitler has given his attack troops flying artillery which covers their advance with a curtain of bombs. This artillery lacks the immense weight of the heavy bombardment and barrage which preceded and accompanied the infantry assaults of 1915–18. It makes up for this deficiency by its sheer "terrifying" power against troops—at least at first—and of course by its mobility. Thus when the tanks are held up they do not have to report back to artillery Headquarters. The air artillery can see the check for themselves. All they have to do is to go and get some more bombs.

These tactics had been thoroughly discussed for many years past and the mechanisation and motorisation of the British Army had been urged notably by the new Chief of Imperial General Staff, General Sir John Dill, by Major General Wavell and Major General Fuller.

The mechanisers were not turned down. The War Office, that is the responsible Government, adopted the Baldwin technique towards this problem which required firm and immediate handling. They accepted mechanisation in principle. The survivors of Dunkirk know what the politicians did in practice.

During the Spanish Civil War, in the battle of the Ebro of 1937, we witnessed the first actual tests of this tank-airplane-motorised infantry. The brave Republican infantry and field artillery simply melted before it. Those who presented these facts to leading politicians in the Government were smiled on with pity and patronisingly told "But these Republican militiamen were only a rabble".

In Poland even the British Government had to notice the military conduct of its ally. It had to observe the

German Army deploy its strength *and its tactics*. These were the tactics of the Ebro, multiplied indeed and diversified. The German armoured columns thrust deep salients into the Polish lines. In vain the Polish cavalry sought to strike against them. The German airplanes detected the Polish concentration and destroyed it. The German flanks were guarded by the German skies. (The Polish Air Force had been obliterated on the ground during the first day.)

The German tanks galloped across the Polish plain and entered Warsaw within ten days. They were driven out, but kept cruising around. In eighteen days the Polish Army was smashed. In London the same men who had made a military alliance with a cavalry army that they could not reach even by sea to reinforce shook their heads and said "What can you expect from Poles?"

What is the answer to the mechanised and motorised army? The first answer, and in the end the final answer, is—another mechanised army. But pending the building of that army of counter-blow what can one do?

The answer is defence-in-depth, which means the abandonment of the archaic idea of "lines" of defence and the adoption of the idea of "zones". This is the tactic whereby you yield the outpost line in order to contest the enemy in the main battle zone or even in the rearward battle zone. This, too, is not "revolutionary". It was all worked out by Colonel von Lossberg in the last war, and by him put to deadly use in the building of the Hindenburg Line in 1916. This tactic of elastic defence has been studied by the British Army for twenty years and young officers in 1939 were lectured on it. But was it employed in the British Zone in Flanders?

Of course the so-called Gort Line had *some* depth. The kind of depth which would have enabled it to stand the infantry assaults of 1918. Unhappily the assaults of 1940 were mechanised.

It is true that the "Gort Line" was never penetrated. It was turned. The French on the right flank let the Germans into "The Bulge". The B.E.F. fell back in orderly retreat from their prepared positions. But the Germans had completely destroyed our rear. Indeed they occupied it. No more shells, supplies or reinforcements could get up to the Army, the Germans were even intercepting the letters to our troops.

The Germans did not cut the B.E.F. off from its communications. They cut off communications from the B.E.F. In fact, the Germans encountered no defence-in-depth. Behind the British Army, either when it had advanced to the line of the Dyle in Belgium itself or when it had retired beyond the Gort Line on the frontier there was no defended "zone". Nor was there any adequate mobile reserve.

But why was there no adequate mobile reserve? Why was there no effective armoured power to strike back against the German thrust? Previous chapters of this book give the answer.

.   .   .   .   .

The story of the campaign is quickly told. Attacked in this war of *three* dimensions by the main Nazi force the Dutch succumbed in four days. They flooded their water lines and appeared ready to defend them. The German parachutists and the Dutch Fifth Columnists broke up their rear.

The next blow fell on Belgium, on the same day. Using aircraft as flying artillery and tanks as cavalry the Germans broke through the first Belgian defence line along the Albert Canal. Southward, they poured armoured divisions through the weakly held Belgian Ardennes Forest.

Next day these troops forced their way across the Meuse and struck deep into France. They quickly transformed the salient they created into a vast bulge. The Maginot-minded French, wedded to the idea of "defensive ferro concrete", did not quickly grasp the danger of this thrust. When they had done so—and the French acted swiftly, firing their Commander in Chief, General Gamelin, together with fifteen generals in a night—the Germans had switched their drive towards the Channel ports. They split the Allied Armies in two. "The Bulge" became the "Gap".

Undeterred by any mechanised power and unchecked by the violent and valiant air assaults of the R.A.F. the Germans swept up the coast and seized the Channel Ports. At this point the Belgian Army capitulated. From then onward the world witnessed probably the most desperate and brilliant rearguard action in military history. Two French divisions covered the retreat and renewed in themselves the glory of Marshal Ney's rearguard which in 1812 had allowed the remnants of the Grande Armée to cross the Beresina and escape the vengeance of the Russians.

On the beaches of Dunkirk a bloodier chapter was enacted. I have told the terrible and wonderful story in the first chapter of this book. By a miracle the greater part of the Army was rescued.

The world gave praise, and England gave prayers of joy at this deliverance. Even then there were not lacking soothsayers to pretend that "defeat had been turned into victory".

Five days later Hitler opened a new offensive against the French Army south of the Somme, now unsupported except by two British divisions. Against them he massed 120 divisions. A third of these were fresh divisions, and at least four of them were armoured. The French opposed them with unsurpassable heroism, but in ten days all solid resistance had been overborne.

The French took toll, indeed. They destroyed hundreds of the thousands of tanks opposing them. Those that fell into their hands bore a familiar sign upon them. They had been made, according to French design, in the Skoda Works of Czechoslovakia.

* * * * *

ON MAY 10TH THE CHAMBERLAIN GOVERNMENT FELL, AND MR. CHURCHILL TOOK POWER. A NEW DETERMINATION AT ONCE BROKE THROUGH. ALREADY, AND AT LONG LAST, THE AEROPLANES, THE TANKS, THE ARMS OF EVERY KIND ARE PILING UP. BUT IN THE MEANTIME THE FRENCH STATE HAS FALLEN UNDER THE CONTROL OF HITLER. AN IMMENSE NEW STRAIN HAS BEEN PLACED ON BRITAIN, AND AN IMMENSE NEW EFFORT IS NOW REQUIRED OF HER.

IN MR. CHURCHILL AS PREMIER, AND IN HIS THREE SERVICE SUPPLY CHIEFS, ERNEST BEVIN, HERBERT MORRISON, AND LORD BEAVERBROOK (TO NAME ONLY FOUR) WE HAVE AN ASSURANCE THAT ALL THAT IS WITHIN THE RANGE OF HUMAN ACHIEVEMENT WILL BE DONE TO MAKE THIS ISLAND "A FORTRESS".

BUT ONE FINAL AND ABSOLUTE GUARANTEE IS STILL IMPERATIVELY DEMANDED BY A PEOPLE DETERMINED TO RESIST AND CONQUER: NAMELY, THAT THE MEN WHO ARE NOW REPAIRING THE BREACHES IN OUR WALLS SHOULD NOT CARRY ALONG WITH THEM THOSE WHO

LET THE WALLS FALL INTO RUIN. THE NATION IS UNITED
TO A MAN IN ITS DESIRE TO PROSECUTE THE WAR IN
TOTAL FORM: THERE MUST BE A SIMILAR UNITY IN THE
NATIONAL CONFIDENCE. LET THE GUILTY MEN RETIRE,
THEN, OF THEIR OWN VOLITION, AND SO MAKE AN
ESSENTIAL CONTRIBUTION TO THE VICTORY UPON WHICH
ALL ARE IMPLACABLY RESOLVED.

READ MORE IN PENGUIN

In every corner of the world, on every subject under the sun, Penguin represents quality and variety – the very best in publishing today.

For complete information about books available from Penguin – including Puffins, Penguin Classics and Arkana – and how to order them, write to us at the appropriate address below. Please note that for copyright reasons the selection of books varies from country to country.

In the United Kingdom: Please write to *Dept. EP, Penguin Books Ltd, Bath Road, Harmondsworth, West Drayton, Middlesex UB7 ODA*

In the United States: Please write to *Consumer Sales, Penguin Putnam Inc., P.O. Box 999, Dept. 17109, Bergenfield, New Jersey 07621-0120.* VISA and MasterCard holders call 1-800-253-6476 to order Penguin titles

In Canada: Please write to *Penguin Books Canada Ltd, 10 Alcorn Avenue, Suite 300, Toronto, Ontario M4V 3B2*

In Australia: Please write to *Penguin Books Australia Ltd, P.O. Box 257, Ringwood, Victoria 3134*

In New Zealand: Please write to *Penguin Books (NZ) Ltd, Private Bag 102902, North Shore Mail Centre, Auckland 10*

In India: Please write to *Penguin Books India Pvt Ltd, 210 Chiranjiv Tower, 43 Nehru Place, New Delhi 110 019*

In the Netherlands: Please write to *Penguin Books Netherlands bv, Postbus 3507, NL-1001 AH Amsterdam*

In Germany: Please write to *Penguin Books Deutschland GmbH, Metzlerstrasse 26, 60594 Frankfurt am Main*

In Spain: Please write to *Penguin Books S. A., Bravo Murillo 19, 1° B, 28015 Madrid*

In Italy: Please write to *Penguin Italia s.r.l., Via Benedetto Croce 2, 20094 Corsico, Milano*

In France: Please write to *Penguin France, Le Carré Wilson, 62 rue Benjamin Baillaud, 31500 Toulouse*

In Japan: Please write to *Penguin Books Japan Ltd, Kaneko Building, 2-3-25 Koraku, Bunkyo-Ku, Tokyo 112*

In South Africa: Please write to *Penguin Books South Africa (Pty) Ltd, Private Bag X14, Parkview, 2122 Johannesburg*

READ MORE IN PENGUIN

Penguin Twentieth-Century Classics offer a selection of the finest works of literature published this century. Spanning the globe from Argentina to America, from France to India, the masters of prose and poetry are represented by the Penguin.

If you would like a catalogue of the Twentieth-Century Classics library, please write to:

Penguin Marketing, 27 Wrights Lane, London W8 5TZ

(Available while stocks last)

READ MORE IN PENGUIN

A CHOICE OF TWENTIETH-CENTURY CLASSICS

Ulysses James Joyce

Ulysses is unquestionably one of the supreme masterpieces, in any artistic form, of the twentieth century. 'It is the book to which we are all indebted and from which none of us can escape' – T. S. Eliot

The Heart of the Matter Graham Greene

Scobie is a highly principled police officer in a war-torn West African state. When he is passed over for promotion he is forced to borrow money to send his despairing wife on holiday. With a duty to repay his debts and an inability to distinguish between love, pity and responsibility to others and to God, Scobie moves inexorably towards his final damnation.

The Age of Innocence Edith Wharton

To the rigid world of propriety, of which Old New York is composed, returns the Countess Olenska. Separated from her European husband and displaying an independence and impulsive awareness of life, she stirs the educated sensitivity of Newland Archer, who is engaged to be married to young May Welland.

Mr Noon D. H. Lawrence

This Penguin edition is the first annotated paperback publication of Lawrence's autobiographical and strikingly innovative unfinished novel. Abandoning a promising academic career, Gilbert Noon becomes embroiled in an affair which causes him to flee to Germany, there to find true passion with the unhappily married wife of an English doctor.

Black List, Section H Francis Stuart

This astonishingly powerful novel follows H on a spiritual quest for revelation and redemption, from his disastrous marriage to Iseult Gonne, the Irish Civil War and internment, to his life as a writer, poultry farmer, racehorse owner and Bohemian in 1930s London, and his arrival in Hitler's Germany in 1940.

READ MORE IN PENGUIN

A CHOICE OF TWENTIETH-CENTURY CLASSICS

Orlando   Virginia Woolf

Sliding in and out of three centuries, and slipping between genders, Orlando is the sparkling incarnation of the personality of Vita Sackville-West as Virginia Woolf saw it.

Selected Poems   Patrick Kavanagh

One of the major figures in the modern Irish poetic canon, Patrick Kavanagh (1904–67) was a post-colonial poet who released Anglo-Irish verse from its prolonged obsession with history, ethnicity and national politics. His poetry, written in an uninhibited vernacular style, focused on the 'common and banal' aspects of contemporary life.

More Die of Heartbreak   Saul Bellow

'One turns the last pages of *More Die of Heartbreak* feeling that no image has been left unexplored by a mind not only at constant work but standing outside itself, mercilessly examining the workings, tracking the leading issues of our times and the composite man in an age of hybrids' – *New York Book Review*

Tell Me How Long the Train's Been Gone   James Baldwin

Leo Proudhammer, a successful Broadway actor, is recovering from a near-fatal heart attack. Talent, luck and ambition have brought him a long way from the Harlem ghetto of his childhood. With Barbara, a white woman who has the courage to love the wrong man, and Christopher, a charismatic black revolutionary, Leo faces a turning-point in his life.

Memories of a Catholic Girlhood   Mary McCarthy

Blending memories and family myths, Mary McCarthy takes us back to the twenties, when she was orphaned in a world of relations as colourful, potent and mysterious as the Catholic religion. 'Superb . . . so heart-breaking that in comparison Jane Eyre seems to have got off lightly' – Anita Brookner